BLUE RIBBON WINNERS
America's Best
STATE FAIR
RECIPES

BLUE RIBBON WINNERS
America's Best
STATE FAIR
RECIPES

Catherine Hanley

SMITHMARK

This edition published in 1993 by SMITHMARK Publishers, Inc., 16 East 32nd Street, New York, NY 10016.

SMITHMARK books are available for bulk purchase for sales promotion and premium use. For details write or call the manager of special sales, SMITHMARK Publishers, Inc., 16 East 32nd Street, New York, NY 10016; (212) 532-6600.

ISBN: 0-8317-0310-5

Printed in the United States of America

10 9 8 7 6 5 4 3 2

Dedication
For Anne, Phyllis and Jim,
who made this all possible

The valuable assistance of the following fair administrators and supervisors made this book possible: Hazel Ashmore, Montgomery, AL; Fran Burcham, Little Rock, AK; Ivy Faulk, Little Rock, AK; Silvia Bishop, Pomona, CA; Sue Belew, Sacramento, CA; Betty Lou Pearson, Beulah, CO; Frank Ross, Tampa, FL; Emma Taylor, Tampa, FL; Merle Miller, Springfield, IL; Jean Stubblefield, Springfield, IL; Marsha Ralston, Indianapolis, IN; Faye Bevelheimer, Indianapolis, IN; Kathie Swift, Des Moines, IA; Arlette Hollister, Des Moines, IA; Dora J. Dutschmann, Hutchinson, KS; Betty Kronish, Louisville, KY; Johnny R. Fatheree, Shreveport, LA; Dr. Norma Roberts, Baton Rouge, LA; Evelyn Hagen, Minneapolis, MN; Mike Heffron, St. Paul, MN; Pattie M. Ryan, Sedalia, MO; Mary Holloway, Sedalia, MO; Dan Fortner, Springfield, MO; Lewis Miller, Springfield, MO; Mary Beth Smith, Springfield, MO; Henry Brandt, Lincoln, NE; Opal Frost, Lincoln, NE; Karlene Pisarcik, Flemington, NJ; Elaine Barbour, Flemington, NJ; M. Steven Anaya, Albuquerque, NM; Marty Bruner, Albuquerque, NM; Sam Rand, Raleigh, NC; Lillian Young, Raleigh, NC; Kandi Reinisch, Minot, ND; Jack Foust, Columbus, OH; Sande Haldiman, Columbus, OH; Sheila Hedlund, Salem, OR; Frederick T. Trump, Bloomsburg, PA; Bettye Templeton, Columbia, SC; Dianne Obr, Huron, SD; Roene Wood, Murray, UT; Ella S. Walker, Monroe, WA; Bonnie Swinney, Snohomish, WA; Julie Carlson, West Allis, WI; Jerelyn Parmelee, South Milwaukee, WI.

My special gratitude to others who were so generous in supplying information or who helped give this book shape: Ann McDuffie, Tampa, FL; Marlene Johnson, Minneapolis, MN; The Pillsbury Company for permission to use Elaine Janas' bread recipe; R. D. Zimmerman, Minneapolis, MN; Merrilyn Tauscher, Byerly's, Minnetonka, MN; Edna Buckley, Collins, NY; Gene Boe, New York, NY; Phyllis McFarland, Salem, OR; Gladys Steinbrecker, West Bend, WI; the exemplary Hennepin County (MN) library system, and particularly to Anne Hanley for those countless hours of typing the manuscript.

CONTENTS

INTRODUCTION

No mean woman can cook well. It calls for a generous spirit, a light hand and a large heart.

Eden Phillpotts

During years of working with food I have been intrigued by what happens when two people make the same recipe with contrasting results. Why does one person turn out a spectacular product and another an indifferent one from the same ingredients? Experience and cooking techniques obviously play a big part. As British author Eden Phillpotts suggests, so does spirit. But how do you convey this information in a recipe?

As I have had opportunities to learn about the women and men who win blue ribbons at the major state fairs, I realized that here you have a large group of people who are consistently achieving extraordinary results with recipes similar to those we all use. What is special about their recipes and what do these cooks do to make the prize-winning difference? That's what every other cook really wants to know and *Blue Ribbon Winners* reveals.

In possibly the only noncommercial cooking contests left, tens of thousands of women and men compete annually in state fair competitions to see who has the best baked goods, pickles and preserves.

The money prizes are modest, not much more than covering the cost of the ingredients. But this is not important. What these good cooks want are the blue ribbons that signify first place.

Blue ribbons from the biggest state and regional fairs in the country are

crumb, lightness and crust. Scoring criteria are remarkably similar from state to state.

In addition to meeting tough judging standards, state fair exhibits are subjected to stress before they ever reach the judges' tables. In a big state like California, entries may have to be mailed in. Even where contestants carefully carry in their contributions, there are delays. Hundreds of entries can't all be judged in one day. So many times food must wait for a day or two before being evaluated.

For good reasons "blue ribbon cooking" has become a synonym for top quality. Recipes for prize-winning food from the fair represent the best in home cooking. So when a blue ribbon or sweepstakes winner is willing not only to share a treasured recipe but will also include tips for success, you can appreciate that the women and men whose recipes are in this book do indeed have generous spirits and large hearts, as well as light hands.

With hundreds of people striving for excellence in competitions as diverse as flower arranging to showing livestock, in addition to culinary arts, fairs are exciting places to visit.

not won easily. Judges often are agricultural extension service home economists or college-level foods teachers, professionals who know how to measure quality and who have been trained to be objective.

Where commercial recipe contests may reflect the preferences and biases of judges or contest sponsors, state fair judging is done "by the book" using scorecards, with a perfect product scoring 100%. Bread, for example, is rated not only on taste and appearance but on texture,

Although state fairs are big business with the largest, Ohio, attracting more than 3.6 million visitors each year, they have managed to retain some of the flavor of the mid-19th century agricultural fairs that were the antecedents for these modern expositions. Fairs still exist "to bring people together to exhibit their best products, to socialize and to observe new methods and products that may improve their lives."

Before I knew much about the kind of people who entered, I assumed that most were rural homemakers, probably women who had won at their county fair and gone to challenge other county winners on the state level.

Now I know that the competition cuts across socio-economic boundaries. In states where the fair is held in a metropolitan area, suburban and urban men and women contestants predominate. They vary in age from the youngest allowed—14 years old in Minnesota—to octogenarians. Many work at full-time jobs, yet manage to bring in dozens of entries, often baking most of the night to get everything ready in time to deliver them by the entry closing hour.

But it was not until I became manager of consumer public relations at Pillsbury and involved in publicizing the Bake-Off contest that I began fully to understand what a special group of people the state fair blue ribbon winners are. The Bake-Off competition differs from most recipe contests because the 100 finalists actually have to prepare their recipes in mini-kitchens set up in a hotel ballroom.

To win the big money awards—$25,000 is the first prize—the contestant first must develop a recipe that is chosen as one of the 100 finalists and then must prepare it for the ultimate judging by a team of savvy food editors from major newspapers and consumer magazines.

After a few times of being an observer on the Bake-Off floor and comparing the contestant's dish as it was taken in to the judges with the food in the photograph we had taken earlier for publicity, it was apparent that some of the finalists were better recipe creators than they were cooks. Indeed, a few were frank about their limited ability in the kitchen. On the other hand, there always were a number of finalists who took all the contest pressure in stride and could turn out cakes, cookies and breads that looked better than our food photographs.

Because my department at Pillsbury obtained biographical information from the finalists, I began to make the connection that those who were frequent blue ribbon winners at state or regional fairs always were in that group of talented, knowledgable cooks who deserved the title of "best cook in town."

Pillsbury also offered special bread baking prizes at several state fairs. This project again involved my interviewing the winners to learn how they achieved their blue ribbon results. It was obvious that they not only had excellent recipes, but that they had developed techniques which make the difference between winning the blue ribbon or the red or white ribbon—or none.

I began to be intrigued with the idea of a cookbook made up of the best of the blue-ribbon recipes plus winners' tips for success. What did these exceptional cooks do that was not written into the recipe? What were the secrets of their culinary achievements?

Now that *Blue Ribbon Winners* has made this idea a reality, it is reasonable to ask if the recipes in it are exactly the same as the winners'. Since the state fair winners sent in recipes using dozens of different recipe styles, they had to be rewritten to follow a more-or-less standard form to make this cookbook easier to use. In some cases the

winner's directions were so helpful that they were written into the recipe, even though it changed the established recipe style.

Generic recipe names were changed. Rolls, for example, became the more descriptive Butterhorn Crescents. Where two entirely different recipes had virtually the

same name, or where the name didn't accurately describe the finished product, they were renamed.

Two places where I had to make small changes in a few recipes were in baking times and recipe yields. I believe that many talented cooks know when food is done without checking baking times, and all of us sometimes are vague about the yield from recipes like cookies.

In some yeast bread recipes I added a range in the amount of flour to accomodate the differences in brands of flour, humidity, etc. In all cases, the recipes were tested with the kind of flour specified. Cake and bread chapters offer guidelines for anyone who wants to substitute.

Anyone who always uses standard contemporary recipes will find that some of the preparation methods in these recipes are unusual. Be assured that the recipe was tested the way the winner sent it in, and the method works. Where I felt reassurance was needed, you will find a comment in the recipe copy or the recipe itself.

In the preserving and pickling chapters, the primary changes were rewriting some of the more complicated recipes to make them easier to follow and standardizing processing methods and times in line with USDA and University of Minnesota methods. For the most part, the processing methods in these recipes were accurate and changes were minor.

Several characteristics of the recipes as a whole were evident: when even a single point can make the critical difference in a judging score, blue ribbon winners depend on traditional baking methods. Many cakes call for creaming the shortening and sugar, separating the eggs and adding the stiffly-beaten egg whites separately and using sifted cake flour. Even muffins often are made by the cake method rather than combining all the ingredients together. Yeast breads can't be hurried. Several recipes specify two rises before the loaves are formed. None calls for fast-acting yeast and nearly all begin by dissolving the yeast in warm water, rather than mixing it with some of the flour.

Does taking this extra time and care pay? Certainly America's best cooks believe it does.

As I was testing the baked products, I began to be aware that I was writing the comments "rich and moist", "keeps well" or "stays fresh for several days" on many of the test sheets. Obviously these are important attributes of recipes that win blue ribbons. Then I understood the reason: these foods not only are made several days before being judged, but they may stand uncovered for several hours and can dry out during the judging. Recipes that retain their freshly-baked qualities longer clearly have a big advantage.

Besides being a good tip for aspiring fair exhibitors, it means that these are useful recipes for those of us who don't have time to bake several times a week.

These blue ribbon recipes are authentic Americana, the time-honored classics and the finest home-style cooking that will survive scores of new eating trends and food fashions. Enjoy them and join me in thanking the gracious, generous-spirited men and women who were willing to share them with us.

PIES & PASTRIES

I f you walk toward the food exhibition area at a state fair and see a cluster of men gathered around one section, you can be sure that is where pies, America's favorite dessert, are displayed. But for all its popularity, homemade pie is a rare treat today in many homes. One reason is lack of time. Equally important is the fact that making pie crust can intimidate even those who consider themselves good cooks.

As the crust can count up to 45 percent in the total score for a two-crust pie, state fair blue ribbon winners obviously are well qualified to offer expert advice. We discovered that several—including a sweepstakes winner—used a version of Never Fail Pie Crust, page 31, that is easy to roll out and can be stored in the refrigerator. With this make-ahead pie dough, it is possible for busy cooks to bake a pie in much less time.

But it is the filling, after all, that defines the pie. So this chapter offers some of America's best recipes for succulent fruit pies, out-of-the-ordinary cream pies, a lemon meringue pie that always cuts perfectly and, as a bonus, Baklava. With these recipes from experts, you'll discover it's easy as pie to make a first rate one.

Butterscotch Pie

When Joy Mers-Lloyd baked her first-ever pie in a ninth grade home economics class, she earned an A for the cherry pie, but her grade was dropped to a B because her work space was so messy. Now she is getting blue ribbons instead of A's, but says she's glad the judges can't grade her kitchen on fair pie baking day. Her Butterscotch Pie has a wonderfully rich, brown sugar flavor, complemented by a whipped cream topping and a garnish of chopped pecans.

1/3 cup flour
1 cup firmly packed brown sugar
1/4 teaspoon salt
2 cups milk
3 egg yolks, slightly beaten
3 tablespoons butter
1/2 teaspoon vanilla extract
1 (9-inch) baked pie shell
1 cup chilled whipping cream
2 tablespoons granulated sugar
1/4 cup chopped pecans

In a medium-size saucepan, mix flour, brown sugar and salt. Add milk. Cook, stirring constantly, over medium heat until mixture thickens and comes to a boil. Cook, stirring constantly, 2 minutes more; remove from heat. Add a small amount of cooked mixture to egg yolks, stirring constantly, then stir egg mixture into cooked mixture. Return to heat and boil 1 minute, stirring constantly. Remove from heat; stir in butter and vanilla. When mixture has cooled slightly, pour into baked pie shell. Cover with plastic wrap and refrigerate at least 2 hours before cutting. In a small bowl, whip cream and granulated sugar. To serve, swirl whipped cream on top of pie; garnish with pecans. Makes 1 (9-inch) pie.

Carol Joy Mers-Lloyd   Galloway, Ohio   Ohio State Fair

Coconut Cream Pie

A talented and creative cook who knows how to make food look as good as it tastes, Joy McAlister turns ordinary coconut cream pie into a beautiful special occasion dessert. The crisp cookie-like crust is a pleasant contrast to the smooth creamy filling. The coconut flavor is enhanced by the addition of coconut extract. Whipped cream is an eye-appealing finishing touch.

2/3 cup granulated sugar
5 tablespoons cornstarch
1/2 teaspoon salt
4 egg yolks
3 cups milk
2 tablespoons butter
1 teaspoon vanilla extract
1 teaspoon coconut extract
1-1/2 cups shredded coconut
1 baked Nut Crust, Double-Layered Chocolate Cream Pie,
   pages 16-17
1 cup whipping cream
1/4 cup powdered sugar

In a medium-size saucepan, combine granulated sugar, cornstarch and salt. In a medium-size bowl, beat egg yolks just enough to combine; mix in milk. Gradually stir into dry ingredients. Cook over medium heat, stirring constantly, until mixture comes to a boil. Cook, stirring constantly, 2 minutes or until mixture is thick. Remove from heat; stir in butter, vanilla, coconut extract and 1 cup of coconut. Cover with plastic wrap to prevent skin from forming and cool. Pour into baked crust, cover and refrigerate until serving time. Preheat oven to 350F (175C). Sprinkle remaining 1/2 cup of coconut on a baking sheet. Bake in preheated oven 15 minutes or until golden brown, stirring several times. In a small bowl, beat whipping cream and powdered sugar until stiff. To serve, spread whipped cream on pie. Sprinkle with toasted coconut. Makes 1 (9-inch) pie.

Joy McAlister Ontario, California   Los Angeles County Fair

Custard Pie

One of the oldest agricultural fairs in the country, the Bloomsburg Fair opened in 1855 with a few displays of fruit and grain. Now this major county fair attracts nearly half a million visitors, more than many state fairs. In an area where excellent pie bakers abound, the display of prize-winning pies is a highlight of the baked products exhibit. Ellen Ebner's traditional recipe for custard pie is flavored with vanilla and nutmeg, if desired. Best served a few hours after baking, it should be refrigerated as soon as the filling has cooled.

4 eggs
1/2 cup sugar
1/2 teaspoon salt
2-1/2 cups milk
1 teaspoon vanilla extract
1/4 teaspoon ground nutmeg, if desired
1 (9-inch) unbaked pie shell with high fluted edge

Preheat oven to 425F (220C). In a medium-size bowl or 1-quart measure, beat eggs just enough to mix. Stir in sugar, salt, milk, vanilla and nutmeg, if desired. Pour into unbaked pie shell. Bake in preheated oven 10 minutes or until crust begins to brown. Reduce temperature to 350F (175C). Bake about 30 minutes more or until knife inserted near edge of filling comes out clean but center is still soft. Makes 1 (9-inch) pie.

Ellen Ebner   Bloomsburg, Pennsylvania   Bloomsburg Fair

Sugar Cream Pie

Sugar Cream Pie is one of the earliest American pies, probably evolving from English chess tarts. A traditional pie in Indiana, it also was the favorite of Joy Mers-Lloyd's Kentucky grandfather. Directions in the earliest "receipts" called for mixing the filling in the unbaked crust, then stirring it with the fingers as it baked. This contemporary version saves fingers from burning by combining the ingredients in a bowl and baking the thick, creamy filling without stirring.

1 cup whipping cream
1 cup half and half
1 cup sugar
1/2 cup flour
1 (9-inch) unbaked pie shell
3 tablespoons butter
1/4 teaspoon ground nutmeg

Preheat oven to 425F (220C). In a medium-size bowl, combine whipping cream, half and half, sugar and flour, beating until well mixed. Pour into unbaked pie shell. Dot with butter; sprinkle with nutmeg. Bake in preheated oven 15 minutes. Remove pie from oven and cover edges of crust with foil to prevent overbrowning. Reduce temperature to 350F (175C). Bake 45 minutes more or until filling thickens, center is bubbly and knife inserted off center comes out clean. Cool before cutting. Makes 1 (9-inch) pie.

Carol Joy Mers-Lloyd   Galloway, Ohio   Ohio State Fair

Double-Layered Chocolate Cream Pie

A self-styled pie fanatic, Joy McAlister has consistently been winning ribbons since she first started entering pies at the fair. She developed her own recipe for this attractive, two-tiered pie which combines a cream cheese layer with chocolate cream filling in a cookie-like crust. To complete this rich party dessert, she pipes whipped cream on top and garnishes it with leaves made by brushing melted chocolate on the back of rose leaves. When set, she carefully peels off the leaves and uses the replicas for decoration.

2 (3-oz.) packages cream cheese,
   room temperature
3/4 cup powdered sugar
3/4 cup whipping cream
2 tablespoons powdered sugar
3/4 cup granulated sugar
1/4 cup cornstarch
6 tablespoons unsweetened cocoa powder
1/4 teaspoon salt
3 egg yolks, slightly beaten
2 cups milk
2 tablespoons butter
1 teaspoon vanilla extract
1 cup whipping cream
1/4 cup powdered sugar
Chocolate leaves or mini-chocolate chips, if desired

Nut Crust:

3/4 cup unbleached all-purpose flour
1/2 cup margarine, softened
1/2 cup chopped walnuts

Prepare Nut Crust. Set aside. In a small bowl, beat cream cheese and 3/4 cup powdered sugar until fluffy. In another small bowl, whip 3/4 cup whipping cream and 2 tablespoons powdered sugar until cream holds stiff peaks. Fold whipped cream into cream cheese mixture. Spread evenly over baked crust. Cover and refrigerate. In a medium-size saucepan, combine granulated sugar, cornstarch, cocoa powder and salt. In a small bowl, combine egg yolks and milk. Slowly add to dry ingredients, stirring to combine. Cook over medium heat, stirring constantly, until mixture comes to a boil. Cook, stirring constantly, 2 minutes or until thick. Remove from heat; stir in butter and vanilla. Cover with plastic wrap to prevent skin from forming and cool. Pour into crust over cream-cheese layer. Cover and refrigerate until serving time. In a small bowl, beat 1 cup whipping cream and 1/4 cup powdered sugar until stiff. To serve, spread with whipped cream. Garnish with chocolate leaves, if desired. Makes 1 (9-inch) pie.

Nut Crust:

Preheat oven to 350F (175C). In a medium-size bowl, using a pastry blender or 2 knives, cut margarine into flour until particles are size of peas. Mix in walnuts. Form dough in a ball. Using fingers, press dough on bottom and up sides of a deep 9-inch pie plate. Bake in preheated oven 15 minutes or until golden. Cool before filling. Makes 1 (9-inch) pie shell.

Joy McAlister   Ontario, California   Los Angeles County Fair

Ribbon Lemon Meringue Pie

Harriett Westman learned to bake lemon meringue pie as a teenager because it was her father's favorite. Over the years she experimented with the basic recipe until she developed one which cuts perfectly, has a fresh lemon flavor without being overly-tart and is topped with a tender "mile high" meringue. Her secret is using twice as many eggs as the standard recipe. Follow her directions and timing precisely to get the same impressive prize-winning results.

1-1/2 cups sugar
3 tablespoons cornstarch
3 tablespoons flour
Dash salt
1-1/2 cups water
6 egg yolks, slightly beaten
1-1/2 teaspoons grated lemon peel
6 tablespoons lemon juice
3 tablespoons butter
6 egg whites, room temperature
1/2 teaspoon cream of tartar
1 (9-inch) baked pie shell
   with high fluted edge
3/4 cup sugar
1 teaspoon vanilla extract

In a medium-size heavy saucepan, mix 1-1/2 cups sugar, cornstarch, flour and salt. Gradually add water, stirring until well blended. Bring mixture to a boil over medium heat, stirring constantly; cook 3 minutes. Remove from heat. Slowly pour about half of mixture into egg yolks, stirring constantly. Slowly pour egg yolk mixture back into hot mixture, stirring constantly. Return saucepan to heat. Bring to a boil, stirring constantly, and cook 3 minutes more. Add lemon peel and juice and butter. Cook about 2 minutes more, stirring with a rubber spatula in a circular motion. Do not let mixture stick to bottom of pan. Filling will be very thick and spatula will leave a track when drawn through filling. Cover saucepan and remove from heat; keep warm. Preheat oven to 350F (175C). In a large bowl, beat egg whites and cream of tartar until foamy. Beat in 3/4 cup sugar, 1 tablespoon at a time. Beat in vanilla with last tablespoon of sugar. Continue beating until egg whites hold a soft peak. Set aside. If filling has cooled, reheat, stirring constantly, before spooning into baked pie shell. Do not let it come to a boil. Spoon hot filling into baked pie shell. Starting around edge of pie, spoon meringue over filling, making sure meringue touches fluting on pie shell. Bake in preheated oven 15 minutes or until meringue is golden brown. Cool about 4 hours at room temperature before cutting.

Makes 1 (9-inch) pie.

TIP   When cutting pie, dip knife into very hot water before each cut.

Harriett Westman   Albuquerque, New Mexico   New Mexico State Fair

Walnut Pie

California's challenge to Southern pecan pie certainly could be Marguerite Jenkins' Walnut Pie. Her old family recipe was judged best of class in pies, besides winning a blue ribbon. Fresh, good-tasting walnuts are essential for this delicious, rich dessert. Slicing the nuts, rather than chopping them, gives the pie a more attractive appearance.

3 eggs
1/2 teaspoon vanilla extract
1/8 teaspoon salt
2/3 cup sugar
1 cup light corn syrup
2 cups sliced walnuts
1 (9-inch) unbaked pie shell

Preheat oven to 350F (175C). In a medium-size bowl, using a wire whisk, beat eggs, vanilla and salt just enough to mix eggs. Stir in sugar and corn syrup, then walnuts. Pour into unbaked pie shell. Bake in preheated oven 50 to 60 minutes or until a knife inserted off center comes out clean, but center is still soft. Makes 1 (9-inch) pie.

Marguerite Jenkins Lodi, California　　　　　　　　California State Fair

Fresh Pear Pie

When you have a surplus of pears ripening at once, one of the most delightful ways to use them is in this spicy, fresh fruit pie, which was judged best of class as well as winning a blue ribbon. Anna Davis' recipe includes apple pie spice, and the juicy pears add their own distinctive flavor and texture.

2 pieces dough, Never Fail Pie Crust, page 31
2-1/2 tablespoons flour
3/4 teaspoon apple pie spice
1/8 teaspoon ground cinnamon
1/8 teaspoon salt
4 cups peeled sliced pears
6 tablespoons brown sugar
1-1/2 teaspoons vanilla extract
1 tablespoon margarine
Water
1 tablespoon milk
2 teaspoons granulated sugar

Preheat oven to 400F (205C). On a lightly floured surface or between 2 pieces waxed paper, roll 1 piece of dough to a 10-inch circle using a lightly floured rolling pin. Line an 8-inch pie plate with rolled dough. Trim, leaving about 1/2-inch overhang. Roll remaining dough to a 9-inch circle; fold in half. Cut small slits along folded edge to allow steam to escape. Set aside. In a small bowl, combine flour, apple pie spice, cinnamon and salt. Gently mix pear slices with flour mixture to coat fruit; mix in brown sugar and vanilla. Turn into pastry-lined pie plate, mounding fruit in middle. Dot with margarine. Lightly brush rim of bottom crust with water. Cover with top crust. Fold top crust under bottom crust and press to seal. Flute edges, brush with milk and sprinkle with granulated sugar. Bake in preheated oven 15 minutes. Reduce temperature to 375F (190C). Bake 25 to 30 minutes more or until crust is brown and juices begin to bubble through slits in pastry. Makes 1 (8-inch) pie.

Anna Davis Fair Oaks, California　　　　　　　　　　California State Fair

Blueberry Pie

Fresh blueberry pie rates high as a Minnesota summer favorite. Most people prefer an uncomplicated filling like Fay Peterson's sweepstakes winner that emphasizes the good fruit flavor. Fair judges also were enthusiastic about her tender, flaky crust. Sometimes called Never Fail Pie Crust, her recipe is from an old collection of home economics teachers' favorite recipes.

2 pieces dough, Never Fail Pie Crust, page 31
2/3 cup sugar
1/4 cup all-purpose flour
1/2 teaspoon ground cinnamon
3 cups fresh blueberries
1 tablespoon butter
Water
Sugar

Preheat oven to 375F (190C). On a lightly floured surface, or between 2 pieces waxed paper, roll 1 piece of dough to a 10-inch circle using a lightly floured rolling pin. Line an 8-inch pie plate with rolled dough. Trim, leaving about 1/2-inch overhang. Roll remaining dough to a 9-inch circle; fold in half. Cut small slits along folded edge to allow steam to escape. Set aside. In a large bowl, combine sugar, flour and cinnamon. Toss lightly with berries. Pour into pastry-lined pie plate. Dot with butter. Brush edge of crust lightly with water. Cover with top crust. Press edges together with tines of a fork. Trim excess crust from edge. Sprinkle with sugar. Bake in preheated oven 45 to 60 minutes or until crust is deep golden brown and juice begins to bubble through slits. Serve slightly warm or at room temperature. Makes 1 (8-inch) pie.

VARIATION Substitute dry pack thawed frozen blueberries for fresh blueberries.

Fay Peterson   Apple Valley, Minnesota   Minnesota State Fair

Sour Cream-Rhubarb Pie

The first cutting of rhubarb traditionally is made into a pie to celebrate the end of winter. Judy Ann Collins' specialty is a mellow, custardy rhubarb pie that appeals even to the minority who are not fond of rhubarb. Her recipe is an adaptation of an aunt's sour cream raisin pie.

3 tablespoons flour
1-1/4 cups sugar
1/2 teaspoon salt
1 egg, beaten
1 cup sour cream
1 teaspoon vanilla extract
1/2 teaspoon lemon extract
3 cups cut-up rhubarb (1/2-inch pieces)
1 (9-inch) unbaked pie shell

Crumb Topping:

1/3 cup sugar
1/3 cup flour
1 teaspoon ground cinnamon
1/4 teaspoon salt
1/4 cup butter, softened.

Preheat oven to 400F (205C). In a large bowl, combine flour, sugar and salt. Stir in egg, sour cream, vanilla and lemon extract; mix well. Fold in rhubarb. Pour into unbaked pie shell. Bake in preheated oven 15 minutes. Reduce temperature to 350F (175C). Bake 25 minutes more. Meanwhile, prepare Crumb Topping. Sprinkle over pie. Bake 15 minutes or until topping is browned. Cool before serving. Makes 1 (9-inch) pie.

Crumb Topping:

In a small bowl, combine all ingredients until crumbly.

Judy Ann Collins   West Des Moines, Iowa   Iowa State Fair

Lattice Crust Peach & Blueberry Pie

As a nutrition-conscious dentist who likes to cook, Ronald Krueger makes fruit pies, experimenting with different combinations of fruit. Fair judges agreed with his wife and three young children that his favorite peach and blueberry pie was a winner and awarded him a blue ribbon in the competitive men only category.

3 cups peeled sliced peaches
1 cup fresh blueberries
2 tablespoons lemon juice
1 cup sugar
2 tablespoons quick-cooking tapioca
1 recipe Basic Pie Crust, Two-Crust (9-inch) Pie Shell, page 34
2 tablespoons butter or margarine

In a large bowl, gently toss fruit with lemon juice, sugar and tapioca to combine. Let stand 15 minutes. Preheat oven to 450F (230C). Prepare Basic Pie Crust as directed. Cut top crust in 1/2-inch strips for lattice top. Spoon fruit mixture into pastry-lined pie plate, mounding it in center. Dot with butter. Arrange lattice strips on top, page 34. Bake in preheated oven about 45 to 50 minutes or until fruit is tender and crust is golden brown. Cool on a wire rack. Serve slightly warm. Makes 1 (9-inch) pie.

Ronald P. Krueger Heath, Ohio   Ohio State Fair

Concord Grape Pie

Ramona Ashburn collects old cookbooks and now owns nearly 500 volumes, with the oldest dating back to 1885. Her grape pie filling is a heirloom family recipe, while her prize-winning pie crust is a variation of Never Fail Pie Crust made with lard and egg yolks, called Tearoom Pastry, page 32. Because Concord grapes have such a short season, she prepares extra filling and freezes it in one-pie amounts for later use.

5 cups rinsed stemmed Concord grapes (about 2 pounds)
1 cup sugar
Dash ground cloves
1/8 teaspoon salt
3-1/2 tablespoons quick-cooking tapioca
2 pieces dough, Tearoom Pastry, page 32
1 tablespoon butter or margarine
1 tablespoon milk
1 teaspoon sugar

Squeeze grapes into a large saucepan. Place skins in a large bowl. Bring pulp to a simmer over medium heat; cook about 5 minutes, stirring a few times. Remove from heat and sieve to remove seeds; discard seeds. Combine pulp with skins. Stir in sugar, cloves, salt and tapioca. Let stand while preparing pastry. Preheat oven to 425F (220C). On a lightly floured surface or between 2 sheets waxed paper, roll 1 piece of dough to an 11-inch circle using a lightly floured rolling pin. Line a 9-inch pie plate with rolled dough. Trim, leaving a 1/2-inch overhang. Roll remaining dough to a 10-inch circle; fold in half. Cut small slits along folded edge to allow steam to escape. Set aside. Pour grape mixture into pastry-lined pie plate. Dot with butter or margarine. Cover with top crust, seal and flute. Brush with milk and sprinkle with sugar. Bake in preheated oven about 30 to 35 minutes or until golden brown and juice bubbles through slits in crust. If edges begin to brown too much, cover with foil. Cool before serving. Makes 1 (9-inch) pie.

Ramona G. Ashburn   Ontario, California   Los Angeles County Fair

Easy Blender Custard Pie

Shirley Dunegan makes her silky-smooth custard pie filling in about one minute in the blender. It is sweeter and richer than traditional custard filling. For best texture, it is important to take the pie out of the oven while the center still quivers when touched. The filling will set as it cools.

2 tablespoons butter, softened
1 cup sugar
1/4 teaspoon salt
6 eggs
1/2 teaspoon ground nutmeg
2 cups milk
1 (9-inch) unbaked pie shell with high fluted edge
Ground nutmeg, if desired

Preheat oven to 450F (230C). Process butter, sugar and salt in a blender at medium speed. With blender running, add eggs, 1 at a time. Adjust blender to low speed and mix in 1/2 teaspoon nutmeg and milk; mixture will be foamy. Pour into unbaked pie shell. Sprinkle with nutmeg, if desired. Bake in preheated oven 10 minutes. Reduce temperature to 325F (165C). Bake 15 minutes more. Remove pie from oven and cover with foil to prevent overbrowning. Bake about 10 minutes more or until knife inserted near edge of filling comes out clean, but center is still soft. Makes 1 (9-inch) pie.

Shirley Dunegan   Malvern, Arkansas   Arkansas State Fair

Baklava

For 36 years Linda Pauls and her husband Ike did custom combining summer to fall, from Texas to Montana. He ran the crew of eight to ten men and she cooked for them. Now that the Pauls are turning the business over to their son, she is home in Kansas and able to compete at the fair. Her blue ribbon Baklava recipe was adapted from one a Texas customer gave her.

4-1/2 cups walnuts, finely ground (about 1 pound)
1-1/2 cups sugar
1/2 teaspoon ground cinnamon
1 pound phyllo pastry sheets
1 pound butter, melted
1-1/2 cups water
1-1/2 cups sugar
1 teaspoon lemon juice

Preheat oven to 300F (150C). Butter bottom of a 15" x 10" x 1-1/2" jelly-roll pan. In a large bowl, combine walnuts, 1-1/2 cups sugar and cinnamon. Lay 1 sheet of phyllo in pan; brush with melted butter. Repeat until 1/2 of phyllo has been used. Sprinkle with walnut mixture to make an even layer of filling. Repeat with layers of remaining phyllo and butter. Using a sharp knife, cut halfway through layers of phyllo in a diamond pattern, making cuts about 1-1/4 inches apart (or width of a ruler). Bake in preheated oven about 1-1/4 hours or until deep golden brown. Meanwhile, in a medium-size saucepan, heat water and 1-1/2 cups sugar over medium heat to boiling, stirring frequently. Reduce heat and simmer 20 minutes. Stir in lemon juice. Remove from heat and cool slightly. Spoon syrup evenly over Baklava. Let stand at room temperature at least 4 hours to absorb syrup before cutting through bottom layer and serving. Makes about 70 pieces.

Linda Pauls   Buhler, Kansas   Kansas State Fair

Wisconsin Cheesecake

Wisconsin ranks first in the country in the production of milk, cheese and butter, so foods made with dairy products rate special categories in state fair competitions. Michelle Klabunde, a student at the University of Wisconsin in Milwaukee, had attended the fair for years and decided she could make a cheesecake as good as ones she had seen on display. The blue ribbon she brought home for her first-time entry proved she was correct. Her cheesecake is rich and dense, with a baked-on topping of slightly sweetened sour cream.

2 (8-oz.) packages cream cheese, room temperature
2/3 cup sugar
3 eggs
1 teaspoon vanilla extract
1 cup sour cream
3 tablespoons sugar

Crust:
20 graham cracker squares, finely crushed
2 tablespoons sugar
6 tablespoons margarine, melted

🏵Prepare Crust. Preheat oven to 350F (175C). In a medium-size bowl, beat cream cheese to soften and blend. Beating continuously, gradually add 2/3 cup sugar, eggs, 1 at a time, and vanilla. Beat about 2 minutes with mixer at medium speed or until creamy and very smooth. Pour filling into chilled crust. Bake in preheated oven 30 to 35 minutes or until filling is almost set. Meanwhile, combine sour cream and 3 table-spoons sugar. Spread over top of cheesecake. Bake 10 minutes more. Cool at room temperature up to 1 hour. Refrigerate several hours or overnight before serving. Store in refrigerator. Makes 12 to 16 servings.

Crust:

In a small bowl, combine graham-cracker crumbs, sugar and marga-rine. Using fingertips, pat an even layer of crumb mixture on bottom and up sides of a 9-inch springform pan. Refrigerate until chilled.

TIP Cheesecake can be made in a deep 9-inch pie pan, although it will be more difficult to serve.

Michelle D. Klabunde   Milwaukee, Wisconsin   Wisconsin State Fair

Chocolate Mousse Eclairs

Kathy Specht has learned that food that looks especially attractive gains extra points from fair judges. So once she has a product that meets all other judging criteria, she concentrates on ways to achieve eye appeal. The 800 blue ribbons and four best of show and sweepstakes awards she has won in the past five years prove her point. When she made eclairs to exhibit, she developed a method to make them impressively high. Her recipe tells how she did it. To gild the lily, her best of show eclairs were filled with a deep-dark chocolate mousse guaranteed to send chocolate lovers into ecstasy.

1/2 cup butter
1 cup water
1 cup sifted all-purpose flour
Dash salt
4 eggs
1 (8-oz.) package cream cheese, room temperature
3/4 cup firmly packed brown sugar
1 (6-oz.) package chocolate chips, melted, cooled
1 egg yolk
1 egg white, beaten until stiff but moist
1 cup whipping cream, whipped
Powdered sugar

Preheat oven to 375F (190C). Grease a baking sheet or line with parchment paper. In a medium-size saucepan, cook butter and water over medium heat until butter is melted and mixture is boiling. In a small bowl, mix flour and salt. Add to boiling mixture. Reduce heat to very low. Stir vigorously until a ball forms in center of pan. Cook 2 minutes more, stirring constantly. Remove from heat; cool a few minutes. Add eggs, 1 at a time, beating constantly. Spoon dough into a pastry bag fitted with a large round tube. To make 6 large eclairs, pipe 6 (3-inch) strips of dough on prepared baking sheet. Then pipe more dough on top of strips 2 more times to build higher eclairs. Bake in preheated oven 40 to 45 minutes or until no beads of moisture show and eclairs are puffed and golden. To make 12 medium-size eclairs, pipe strips of dough about 4 inches long and 1 inch wide. Bake in preheated oven about 30 minutes or until no beads of moisture show and eclairs are puffed and golden. Turn off oven. Using a sharp knife, cut a tiny slit in sides of pastry. Return to oven; let stand 15 minutes to dry. Remove to a wire rack to cool. To make filling, in a medium-size bowl, beat cream cheese, brown sugar, chocolate chips and egg yolk until smooth and well blended. Fold in egg white and whipped cream. Pipe or spoon filling into cooled eclairs. Dust with powdered sugar. Makes 6 large or 12 medium-size eclairs.

Kathy Specht   Carlsbad, California   California State Fair

Never Fail Pie Crust

3 cups all-purpose flour
1 teaspoon salt
1-1/4 cups shortening
1 egg, beaten
5 tablespoons cold water
1 tablespoon vinegar

In a large bowl, mix flour and salt. Using a pastry blender, 2 knives or fingertips, cut in shortening until well-blended. In a 1-cup liquid measure, combine egg, water and vinegar. Add all at once to flour mixture, blending with a spoon or fork until flour is moistened. Divide evenly in 3 pieces. Pat out 1 piece on a lightly floured surface or between 2 pieces waxed paper. Using a lightly floured rolling pin, roll dough to a 10-inch circle. Carefully transfer to an 8-inch pie plate. Repeat with remaining dough or wrap in plastic wrap and refrigerate up to 2 weeks or freeze. Makes pastry for 1 two-crust (8-inch) pie and 1 (8-inch) pie shell or 3 (8-inch) pie shells.

TIP   If unbleached flour is used, dough will darken after refrigerating a few days. This will not hurt eating quality of crust. Freezing will prevent darkening. A pliable dough that is easy to roll out, this can be patched and even rerolled without getting tough. The baked crust is tender, flaky and crisp.

room Pastry

5 cups all-purpose flour
4 teaspoons sugar
1/2 teaspoon salt
1/2 teaspoon baking powder
1-1/2 cups lard
2 egg yolks
Cold water

In a large bowl, combine flour, sugar, salt and baking powder. Using a pastry blender, 2 knives or fingertips, cut in lard until mixture is crumbly. Beat egg yolks slightly in a liquid measuring cup. Add enough cold water to make 1 cup liquid. Pour into flour and lard mixture. Using a fork, stir until dough forms a ball and cleans sides of bowl. Divide dough evenly in 4 pieces. Pat out 1 piece on a lightly floured surface or between 2 pieces waxed paper. Using a lightly floured rolling pin, roll dough to a 10-inch circle. Carefully transfer to an 8-inch pie plate. Repeat with remaining dough or wrap extra pieces in foil and freeze. Makes pastry for 2 two-crust (8-inch) pies or 4 (8-inch) pie shells.

TIP Lard makes a very tender, flaky pie crust with a flavor that complements fruit pies. Make sure the lard you buy is fresh. The best lard has a mild flavor.

Basic Pie Crust

     This is the pastry dough used for most blue ribbon pies. While a majority of winners use vegetable shortening, a few prefer part lard. You can also use part butter or margarine for flavor, as long as you follow the basic proportion of 1/3 cup fat to 1 cup all-purpose flour. (High protein bread flour and cake flour will not produce as good results.) Since you do *not* want to develop the gluten in the flour when you make pie crust, it is important not to "work" the dough too much when mixing and rolling it out. Overhandling will toughen the crust, and it will be less flaky. Standard cookbook recipes call for 1-1/2 cups of flour for a 9-inch pie shell. However, prize winning one-crust pies nearly always have a high, built-up crust, requiring closer to 2 cups flour. On that basis, you will need 3 cups flour for pastry for a two-crust 9-inch pie. When the crust can count for 25 to 45 percent of the pie score, state fair winners know it doesn't pay to skimp.

One-Crust (9-inch) Pie Shell

2 cups all-purpose flour
1/2 teaspoon salt
2/3 cup vegetable shortening
5 to 6 tablespoons ice water

Preheat oven to 425F (220C). In a large bowl, mix flour and salt. Using a pastry blender, 2 knives or fingertips, cut in shortening until flour is well mixed with fat and mixture is crumbly. Sprinkle with water, a little at a time, stirring with a fork, until dough holds together. Dryness of flour and humidity will affect amount of water needed. Form dough in a ball. Pat out on lightly floured surface or between 2 pieces waxed paper. Using a lightly floured rolling pin, roll dough to an 11-inch circle about 1/8 inch thick. Fold dough in half; carefully transfer to pie plate without stretching. Trim edges evenly, leaving about a 1-inch overhang. Fold this under itself all around to make a ridge; flute edge. Using a fork, prick shell over bottom and sides. Bake in preheated oven about 15 minutes or until crisp and golden brown. For an unbaked shell, follow recipe directions.

Two-Crust (9-inch) Pie Shell

3 cups all-purpose flour
1/2 teaspoon salt
1 cup vegetable shortening
7 to 8 tablespoons ice water

In a large bowl, mix flour and salt. Using a pastry blender, 2 knives or fingertips, cut in shortening until flour is well mixed with fat and mixture is crumbly. Sprinkle with water a little at a time, stirring with a fork, until dough holds together. Dryness of flour and humidity will affect amount of water needed. Divide dough in 2 pieces, using a little more than half for bottom crust. Pat out bottom crust on a lightly floured surface or between 2 pieces waxed paper. Using a lightly floured rolling pin, roll dough to an 11-inch circle about 1/8 inch thick. Fold dough in half; carefully transfer to pie plate without stretching. Trim edge evenly, leaving about 1/2 inch overhang. Roll top crust to a 10-inch circle. Fold dough in half. Cut small slits along folded edge to allow steam to escape. Lightly brush edge of bottom crust with water. Arrange top crust over filling. Trim top crust to 1/2-inch overhang. Press top and bottom crust edges together. Fold overhang under itself and flute edge or press tines of a fork around edge. Bake according to recipe directions.

Lattice Top

Cut top crust in 1/2-inch-wide strips. Place 1/2 of strips over filling, using longest ones in center. Weave remaining strips through first strips. Trim edges. Fold overhang under itself and flute edge.

TIP In very hot weather, chilling dough will make it easier to roll. Dough also can be made in advance, well wrapped and refrigerated for several hours or overnight.

FAMILY & PARTY CAKES

I n an era of cake mixes and quick mix cakes, it is encouraging
to discover that the art of baking light, velvety-textured layer
cakes, jelly-rolls and airy chiffon cakes is alive and thriving
among exhibitors at state fairs across the country.

Although food experts are partially correct in saying we have lost
a generation of bakers, state fair judges could point out that this
may be changing. This collection of blue ribbon winners includes a
teenager, a college student, several young working women and a
young man, all of whom represent a new generation of cake bakers.

Southern women have always had a reputation for excelling as
cake bakers, so many of these recipes show Southern roots:
poundcake, jam cake, Lane Cake, Black Walnut Layer Cake, Cola
Cake and Robert E. Lee Cake.

In state fair judging, flavor scores the highest number of points,
followed by appearance. In addition, to win the top prize, the cake
must rate tops on tenderness, lightness, moistness and texture.
Whether you are looking for a homey gingerbread or an impressive
party cake, you will find it here.

Changing Pan Sizes

Fair winners know that a gorgeous frosted layer cake can score extra points with judges on appearance, so many of these blue ribbon cakes are baked in layers. If you prefer, the batter can be baked in a 13" x 9" pan. Bundt pound cakes also can be baked in two 9" x 5" loaf pans. If you have 8-inch-round cake pans and the recipe specifies 9-inch-round cake pans, you can bake the extra batter as cupcakes.

Pan Preparation

Nothing is more disappointing than to take perfect looking layers or a Bundt cake out of the oven, then have a piece stick to the pan when you turn it out. To help prevent this, most butter cake recipes call for greasing (solid shortening, not oil) and flouring the pans, then letting the cake cool in the pan for a designated time before removing it. This allows the structure of the cake to set, so it will not crack or break. It also is helpful to gently loosen the cake around the edge of the pan before removing it.

Flour Tips

Cake flour is a good choice for very delicate, fine-grained, butter cakes. For most others, all-purpose flour performs well and is preferred for sturdier cakes like applesauce cake. As each cake in this chapter has won a blue ribbon or higher award at a major fair, the recipe calls for the kind of flour specified by the winner.
If you want to substitute another flour for the flour in any of the recipes, use the following formula:

   1 cup all-purpose flour = 1 cup
      plus 2 tablespoons cake flour
   1 cup cake flour = 1 cup minus 2 tablespoons all-purpose flour
   Do not substitute self-rising, bread or instant-blending flour in
      any of these recipes.

It is important to follow specific recipe directions for measuring flour. Older recipes almost always called for sifting flour before measuring. Contemporary ones are more likely to skip that step. In a large cake recipe, the difference in measurement between 3 cups of sifted and unsifted flour is about 1/4 cup, enough to significantly effect baking results.

Taking the Mystery Out of White Chocolate

The Food and Drug Administration's official "standard of identity" for chocolate states that the product must contain both cocoa butter and chocolate liquor, which gives it the brown color. So the confection Europeans call white chocolate legally cannot be labeled chocolate when it is produced in the United States.

So when the recipe calls for white chocolate, how do you find it?

Some chocolate shops that make their own candy or stores that carry candymaking supplies will sell it unlabeled in chunks. If your only source is a food store, look in the section that sells the large, fine-quality bars of chocolate candy. You may find one or two European bars that *are* labeled white chocolate. Others will have a trade name with "white" in it. Read the label to make sure that cocoa butter is an ingredient.

Some of the white chocolate bars also contain ground or finely chopped nuts. If the nuts are compatible with the recipe, these can be used. Keep in mind that some of the weight of the bar is nuts, so you will need to use a little more of this chocolate.

White confectioner's coating or almond bark may be erroneously referred to as white chocolate. These products, used principally in candy making or for cake decorating, are made with palm kernel or coconut oil rather than cocoa butter. They usually are found in the baking section in grocery stores. While these products can be substituted for white chocolate in many recipes, they do not have the same delicate flavor.

Caramel Cake

A nurse who loves to cook, Harriet Holley also finds time to help a caterer with weddings. When she decided to try her luck competing in the state fair two years ago, she brought home four blue ribbons and the sweepstakes prize for Caramel Cake. Her layer cake combines a traditional Southern butter cake recipe with a cooked caramel frosting thickened with powdered sugar. The rich cake has a wonderful buttery flavor and stays fresh for several days.

> 2-1/2 cups all-purpose flour
> 3/4 teaspoon baking soda
> 3/4 teaspoon salt
> 1 cup butter, softened
> 2 cups sugar
> 1 teaspoon vanilla extract
> 3 eggs
> 1 cup buttermilk
>
> *Caramel Frosting:*
>
> 1/2 cup margarine
> 1 cup firmly packed dark-brown sugar
> 1/2 cup milk
> 1 teaspoon vanilla extract
> About 4 cups powdered sugar

Preheat oven to 350F (175C). Generously grease and flour 2 (9-inch) round cake pans. In a medium-size bowl, mix flour, baking soda and salt. In a large bowl, cream butter. Gradually add sugar and vanilla, beating until mixture is fluffy. Add eggs, 1 at a time, beating well after each addition. Add flour mixture alternately with buttermilk. Divide batter evenly between prepared pans. Bake in preheated oven about 30 to 35 minutes or until a wooden pick inserted into center comes out clean. Cool in pans on a wire rack 10 minutes. Remove from pans; cool completely. Prepare Caramel Frosting. Spread about 1/3 of frosting between layers. Frost sides and top of cake with remaining frosting. Makes 1 (9-inch) 2-layer cake.

Caramel Frosting:

In a medium-size saucepan, melt margarine. Stir in brown sugar and milk. Bring to a boil and simmer 5 minutes, stirring constantly. Remove from heat. Add vanilla. Gradually beat in powdered sugar until frosting reaches spreading consistency. Use while still warm; cooled frosting is stiff and hard to spread.

Harriet C. Holley   W. Columbia, South Carolina   South Carolina State Fair

Black Walnut Layer Cake

American Black Walnut trees are cultivated in Missouri both for their beautiful dark lumber and for the distinctively flavored nuts. To recognize the commercial importance of the trees, in 1986 the Missouri State Fair added a new class for black walnut cakes. In addition to a special prize, the blue ribbon cake was presented to the governor. Brenda Danuser's first prize winner, an old family recipe, is an elegant, rich, three-layer cake made with buttermilk and five eggs. She adds a cream cheese filling and frosting and decorates the top with black walnuts and coconut.

2 cups all-purpose flour
1 teaspoon baking soda
1/4 teaspoon salt
1/2 cup margarine
1/2 cup shortening
2 cups sugar
5 eggs, separated
1 cup buttermilk
1 teaspoon vanilla extract
1-1/2 cups chopped black walnuts
1 cup shredded coconut
1/2 teaspoon cream of tartar
1/2 cup shredded coconut
1/2 cup chopped black walnuts

Cream Cheese Frosting:

1/2 cup margarine, room temperature
1 (8-oz.) package cream cheese, room temperature
1 teaspoon vanilla extract
3-1/2 cups powdered sugar

🎗 Preheat oven to 350F (175C). Generously grease and flour 3 (9-inch) round cake pans. In a medium-size bowl, mix flour, baking soda and salt. In a large bowl, combine margarine and shortening. Add sugar; beat until smooth and well-blended. Add egg yolks to creamed mixture; beat 2 minutes. Add flour mixture alternately with buttermilk to creamed mixture, beginning and ending with flour, beating until batter is smooth and well-blended. Stir in vanilla, 1-1/2 cups black walnuts and 1 cup coconut. Using clean beaters, in a medium-size bowl, beat egg whites and cream of tartar until stiff but moist and peaks form. Gently fold egg whites into batter. Divide batter evenly between prepared pans. Bake in preheated oven 30 minutes or until a wooden pick inserted into center comes out clean. Cool in pans on wire racks 10 minutes. Remove from pans; cool completely. Prepare Cream Cheese Frosting. Spread top of 1 layer with frosting. Place second layer on top; spread with frosting. Place third layer on top. Frost top of cake. Sprinkle top with 1/2 cup coconut and garnish with 1/2 cup black walnuts. Makes 1 (9-inch) 3-layer cake.

Cream Cheese Frosting:

In a medium-size bowl, cream margarine, cream cheese and vanilla until well-blended. Beat in powdered sugar until mixture is fluffy and well-blended.

VARIATION If black walnuts are not available, substitute black walnut extract for vanilla and use chopped California walnuts.

Brenda Danuser   Montreal, Missouri   Missouri State Fair

Orange Delight Cake

Combine light, delicately-flavored orange cake layers with a tangy, orange filling and a melt-in-the-mouth frosting that looks like whipped cream. Add Irene Losey's talent as a cake baker and you have a winner, as she has found every time she has entered this cake at a fair. The unusual frosting will make a big hit with anyone who doesn't care for overly sweet white frosting. The method is unusual; you first make a thick sauce and then beat that into a fluffy butter and sugar mixture. The secret of the whipped cream texture is long beating with an electric mixer. This frosting stays soft and creamy and is easy to spread in attractive swirls.

2-1/2 cups cake flour
3-1/2 teaspoons baking powder
1/2 teaspoon salt
3 eggs, separated, room temperature
3/4 cup shortening
1-1/2 cups sugar
1 tablespoon grated orange peel
1 cup cold freshly-squeezed orange juice including pulp

Orange Filling:

1/4 cup cornstarch
1 cup sugar
1/2 teaspoon salt
1 cup freshly-squeezed orange juice including pulp
1 tablespoon lemon juice
2 tablespoons finely grated orange peel
2 tablespoons butter

Whipped Cream Frosting:

1 cup milk
1/4 cup all-purpose flour
1 cup butter, softened
1 cup sugar
2 teaspoons finely grated orange peel

Preheat oven to 350F (175C). Grease and flour 2 (9-inch) round cake pans. Line pan bottoms with waxed paper. Sift flour, baking powder and salt into a medium-size bowl. In another medium-size bowl, beat egg whites until stiff but still moist. Without washing beaters, in a small bowl, beat yolks until thick and lemon colored. In a large bowl, cream shortening and sugar until fluffy and well-blended. Add orange peel and beaten egg yolks; mix well. By hand or with slowest mixer speed, add dry ingredients alternately with orange juice. Do not overmix. Fold in stiffly-beaten egg whites just until they are blended. Divide batter evenly between prepared pans. Bake in preheated oven 30 to 35 minutes or until a wooden pick inserted into center comes out clean. Cool in pans on a wire rack 10 minutes. Turn out on wire rack and remove waxed paper. Cool right side up. Prepare Orange Filling and Whipped Cream Frosting. Spread filling between layers. Frost sides and top of cake with frosting. Makes 1 (9-inch) 2-layer cake.

Orange Filling:

In a heavy saucepan, mix cornstarch, sugar and salt. Gradually stir in orange and lemon juice. Cook over medium heat, stirring constantly, until mixture thickens and boils. Boil 1 minute, stirring constantly, or until very thick. Remove from heat; stir in orange peel and butter. Cool to room temperature.

Whipped Cream Frosting:

In a small saucepan, blend milk and flour. Cook over medium heat, stirring constantly, until mixture boils. Cook about 1 minute more, stirring constantly, or until mixture is like a thick white sauce. Cool. In a medium-size bowl, beat butter, sugar and orange peel until fluffy. Add cooled milk mixture and beat with an electric mixer at high speed 3 to 5 minutes or until frosting is very light and fluffy and resembles whipped cream.

TIP   To retain delicate flavor of this cake, use only orange part of peel. Do not use any bitter-flavored white part of peel.

Irene Losey   Portland, Oregon   Oregon State Fair

Lane Cake

When Paulette Van de Zande's son won a blue ribbon at the big Los Angeles County Fair using one of her cake recipes, she decided if he could win, so could she, although she had never entered state fair competition before. Since the North Carolina State Fair takes place a month later than the California event, both mother and son were able to win blue ribbons on opposite sides of the country. Lane Cake traditionally is reserved for Christmas or other celebrations.

1 cup butter or butter and part margarine, softened
2 cups sugar
3-1/4 cups sifted all-purpose flour
2 teaspoons baking powder
1 cup milk
1 teaspoon vanilla extract
8 egg whites, beaten until stiff but moist

Lane Filling:

1/2 cup butter or butter and part margarine, softened
1 cup sugar
8 egg yolks, beaten
1 cup golden raisins, chopped
1 cup chopped pecans
1 teaspoon vanilla extract

Fluffy White Frosting:

2-1/2 cups sugar
1/8 teaspoon salt
1/3 cup light corn syrup
2/3 cup water
2 egg whites
1 teaspoon vanilla extract

Preheat oven to 350F (175C). Grease and flour 3 (9-inch) round cake pans. Line pan bottoms with waxed paper; grease waxed paper. In a large bowl, cream butter; gradually add sugar and beat until light and very well blended. Sift part of flour and baking powder into batter; mix until well blended. Alternately, add milk and vanilla with remaining flour, mixing after each addition. Carefully fold in beaten egg whites. Divide batter evenly among prepared pans. Bake in preheated oven about 30 minutes or until golden and a wooden pick inserted into center comes out clean. Cool in pans on wire racks 10 minutes. Turn out, remove waxed paper and cool completely. Prepare Lane Filling and Fluffy White Frosting. Spread top of 1 layer with filling. Place second layer on top; spread with filling. Place third layer on top. Frost sides and top of cake with warm frosting. Makes 1 (9-inch) 3-layer cake.

Lane Filling:

In top of a large double boiler, cream butter and sugar until well-blended. Beat in egg yolks. Cook over simmering water, stirring constantly, until thick. Remove from heat and stir in raisins, pecans and vanilla. Cool to room temperature.

Fluffy White Frosting:

In a medium-size saucepan, combine sugar, corn syrup, water and salt. Boil over medium heat, without stirring, until mixture reaches 225F (105C). Immediately, using an electric mixer, beat egg whites until stiff in a large bowl. When syrup reaches 240F (115C), remove from heat. Slowly pour syrup in a steady stream over stiffly beaten whites, continuing to beat egg whites at high speed until frosting is glossy. Beat at medium speed until frosting is stiff enough to hold peaks; beat in vanilla. Use while frosting is still slightly warm and easy to spread.

TIP If cake is not to be served same day it is assembled, cover *loosely* with foil or waxed paper. Store at room temperature up to 2 days.

Paulette Van de Zande   Raleigh, North Carolina   North Carolina State Fair

Perfect Spice Cake

Janice Livelsberger first exhibited in the junior division of the Los Angeles County Fair when she was in third grade. As a college senior, she's a veteran of major fair competitions who bakes for fun and considers it an exciting hobby. Her spice cake combines three rich-flavored, tender cake layers with a fluffy brown sugar version of seven-minute frosting.

2-1/4 cups sifted cake flour
1 teaspoon baking powder
1 teaspoon salt
1 teaspoon ground cinnamon
3/4 teaspoon baking soda
1/4 teaspoon ground cloves
Dash pepper
3/4 cup shortening
1 cup sugar
3/4 cup firmly packed
    dark-brown sugar
3 eggs
1 teaspoon vanilla
    extract
1 cup buttermilk

Sea Foam Frosting:

2 egg whites
1-1/2 cups firmly packed
    brown sugar
1/3 cup water
1 teaspoon vanilla extract

Preheat oven to 350F (175C). Generously grease and flour 3 (9-inch) round cake pans. Sift flour, baking powder, salt, cinnamon, baking soda, cloves and pepper into a medium-size bowl. In a large bowl, cream shortening and sugars until light and fluffy. Add eggs, 1 at a time, beating well after each addition. Beat in vanilla. Add dry ingredients alternately with buttermilk, beating after each addition until well blended. Divide batter evenly among prepared cake pans. Bake in preheated oven 25 minutes or until a wooden pick inserted into center comes out clean. Cool in pans on wire racks 10 minutes. Remove from pans; cool on wire racks. Prepare Sea Foam Frosting. Spread top of 1 layer with frosting. Place second layer on top; spread with frosting. Place third layer on top. Frost sides and top of cake. Makes 1 (9-inch) 3-layer cake.

Sea Foam Frosting:

In top of a large double boiler, combine egg whites, brown sugar and water. Set over simmering (not boiling) water and beat with an electric mixer about 7 minutes or until soft peaks form. Remove from heat. Add vanilla; continue to beat until thick enough to spread.

Janice Livelsberger Glendora, California   Los Angeles County Fair

Arkansas Blackberry Jam Cake

Jam cake is one of the great Southern recipes with many variations from state to state. The most elaborate is a complicated holiday version filled with nuts, dried and candied fruit and coconut. Shirley Dunegan prefers her more basic recipe. A rich, spicy layer cake, Arkansas Blackberry Jam Cake stays fresh for days and makes a delectable dessert for family or guests. The traditional filling and frosting stays soft and helps keep the cake moist. An active member of Arkansas Extension Homemakers, Mrs. Dunegan was the 1985 Arkansas Homemaker of the Year.

2-3/4 cups all-purpose flour
1 teaspoon baking soda
1 teaspoon allspice
1 teaspoon ground cloves
1 teaspoon ground cinnamon
3/4 cup butter or margarine, softened
2 cups sugar
4 eggs, separated
3/4 cup buttermilk
1 cup blackberry jam or jelly

Creamy Filling & Frosting:

3/4 cup butter, softened
1 cup sugar
2 eggs
1 tablespoon cornstarch
1-1/2 cups milk

🏵 Preheat oven to 350F (175C). Generously grease and flour 3 (9-inch) round cake pans. In a medium-size bowl, mix flour, baking soda and spices. In a large bowl, cream butter; add sugar and beat until mixture is fluffy. In a small bowl, beat egg yolks until lemon colored; add to creamed mixture. Add buttermilk and jam; beat until thoroughly blended. Stir in flour mixture. In a small bowl, beat egg whites until stiff but still moist. Fold into batter. Divide batter evenly among prepared cake pans. Bake in preheated oven about 35 to 40 minutes or until a wooden pick inserted into center comes out clean. Cool in pans on wire racks 10 minutes. Remove from pans; cool completely. Spread top of 1 layer with filling. Place second layer on top; spread with filling. Place third layer on top. Frost sides and top of cake. Makes 1 (9-inch) 3-layer cake.

Creamy Filling & Frosting:

In top of a double boiler, cream butter and sugar; beat in eggs. Stir in cornstarch and milk. Set over simmering water. Cook, stirring constantly, about 10 minutes or until filling is consistency of a thick pudding. Cool to room temperature.

VARIATION Shirley Dunegan sometimes replaces Cream Filling & Frosting with blackberry jam. Melt blackberry jam and drizzle between layers and over top of cake, letting it run down sides.

TIP Cake will stay fresh for several days in refrigerator.

Shirley Dunegan   Malvern, Arkansas   Arkansas State Fair

Allen's Chocolate Poundcake

Amy Jackson's chocoholic husband Allen is her official taster. At his suggestion, she substituted buttermilk for part of the liquid in her original chocolate poundcake. Between them, they developed a winner that was awarded a blue ribbon the first time she entered the state fair, competing against Deep South poundcake experts.

3 cups all-purpose flour
1/2 teaspoon baking powder
1/2 teaspoon salt
1/2 cup unsweetened cocoa powder
1/2 cup shortening
1 cup butter, softened
3 cups sugar
5 eggs, room temperature
1 teaspoon vanilla extract
1/2 cup milk
3/4 cup buttermilk

Preheat oven to 325F (165C). Generously grease and flour a 10-inch tube pan. Sift flour, baking powder, salt and cocoa powder into a medium-size bowl. In a large bowl, cream shortening and butter to blend; gradually add sugar, beating until light and fluffy. Add eggs, 1 at a time, beating well after each addition. Add vanilla. Alternate flour mixture, milk and buttermilk, beating until batter is smooth and well-blended. Pour batter into prepared pan. Bake in preheated oven 1-1/4 hours or until a wooden pick inserted into center comes out clean. Cool in pan on a wire rack 15 minutes. Invert on a serving plate. Cool completely before serving. Makes 1 (10-inch) tube cake.

Amy A. Jackson   Gilbert, South Carolina   South Carolina State Fair

Orange-Glazed Poundcake

Lucille Hansen insists on the best quality ingredients, knowing that flavor is all-important. Buttermilk gives a tender crumb, and orange peel adds a refreshing citrus flavor.

3 cups sifted all-purpose flour
1/2 teaspoon baking soda
1/2 teaspoon baking powder
1/2 teaspoon salt
1 cup butter, room temperature
2 cups sugar
4 eggs, room temperature
1/2 teaspoon vanilla extract
4 teaspoons grated orange peel, orange part only
1 cup buttermilk

Glaze:
1 cup powdered sugar
1 to 2 tablespoons orange juice

Preheat oven to 325F (165C). Generously grease and flour a 10-inch tube or Bundt pan. Sift flour, baking soda, baking powder and salt into a medium-size bowl. In a large bowl, cream butter. Add sugar and beat until light and fluffy. Add eggs, 1 at a time, and beat until batter is light and fluffy. Stir in vanilla and orange peel. Alternate dry ingredients and buttermilk and beat until batter is smooth and well-blended. Pour into prepared pan. Bake in preheated oven 55 to 65 minutes or until a wooden pick inserted into center comes out clean. Cool in pan on a wire rack 10 minutes. Remove from pan; cool completely. Prepare Glaze; drizzle over cake. Makes 1 (10-inch) pound cake.

Glaze:

In a small bowl, combine powdered sugar and enough orange juice to make a spoonable glaze.

Lucille Hansen   Flanagan, Illinois   Illinois State Fair

White Chocolate-Coconut Cake

The "favorite cake" category is one of the most competitive in the culinary arts department at the Kentucky State Fair. Martha York wondered if she would have a chance at any of the ribbons as she counted up 42 other beautiful entries. But after an hour of sampling and scoring, the judges tagged her lavish, three-layer white chocolate cake with the blue ribbon. Definitely a special occasion dessert, the white cake is rich with coconut and almonds, filled and frosted with whipped cream and garnished with coconut and curls of white chocolate. She strongly advises using real white chocolate, not confectioner's coating (almond bark) for best flavor. See Taking the Mystery out of White Chocolate, page 37. In the South frozen coconut is popular as a substitute for fresh coconut. If it is not available, use the moist canned flaked coconut. Although melted chocolate will harden if a few drops of water get into it, her method of melting the white chocolate in water *does* work.

> 5 to 6 ounces white chocolate
> 1/2 cup water
> 4 egg whites
> 2 cups sugar
> 1 cup butter, room temperature
> 2-1/2 cups all-purpose flour
> 1-1/2 teaspoons baking powder
> 1/2 teaspoon salt
> 1 cup buttermilk
> 1 cup blanched almonds, chopped fine
> 1 (3-1/2-oz.) can flaked coconut (about 1-1/3 cups)
> 1/2 cup raspberry jam
> White chocolate curls
> 1 (6-oz.) package frozen coconut (about 2 cups)

> *Whipped Cream Frosting:*
> 2 cups whipping cream, chilled
> 2 tablespoons powdered sugar

Preheat oven to 350F (175C). Generously grease and flour 3 (9-inch) round cake pans. Break or chop white chocolate in small pieces. Melt with water in top of double boiler set over hot water, stirring occasionally. Cool. In a medium-size bowl, beat egg whites until soft peaks form. Gradually beat in 1/2 cup of sugar; continue beating to form stiff shiny peaks. Set aside. Without washing beaters, in a large bowl, cream remaining 1-1/2 cups of sugar and butter until light and fluffy. Sift flour, baking powder and salt into another medium-size bowl. Add dry ingredients alternately with buttermilk and white chocolate mixture, beginning and ending with flour. Fold in almonds and coconut, then fold in egg whites. Divide batter evenly among prepared pans. Bake in preheated oven 30 to 35 minutes or until a wooden pick inserted into center comes out clean. Cool cake in pans about 5 minutes. Remove from pans and cool completely on wire racks. Split one layer in half horizontally. Spread bottom half with raspberry jam. Replace top half; use as middle layer of cake. Prepare Whipped Cream Frosting. Spread frosting between layers and on top and sides of cake. Garnish with white chocolate curls and gently pat coconut onto sides of cake. Cover cake loosely and refrigerate. Makes 1 (9-inch) 3-layer cake.

Whipped Cream Frosting:

In a medium-size bowl, beat cream with sugar until stiff.

TIP Make white chocolate curls by pulling vegetable peeler across surface of slightly-warmed chocolate or make curly shreds using shredding side of grater.

Martha York   Louisville, Kentucky   Kentucky State Fair

Chocolate Fudge Cake

Helen Rushton spent 10 years as a 4-H Club leader while her daughters were involved in those activities. Then she decided her time to take part in fair activities had arrived. For more than three decades she has been winning ribbons and sweepstakes awards at the Indiana State Fair, concentrating in recent years on all kinds of baking. Her chocolate cake combines deep, rich color and fudgy flavor with the lighter texture of a devil's food cake. Fill and frost it with any favorite chocolate frosting.

3 cups sifted cake flour
1-1/2 teaspoons baking soda
3/4 teaspoon salt
3/4 cup butter or margarine, softened
2-1/4 cups sugar
1-1/2 teaspoons vanilla extract
3 eggs
3 (1-oz.) squares unsweetened baking chocolate, melted
1-1/2 cups ice water
1 teaspoon red food coloring, if desired

Preheat oven to 350F (175C). Generously grease and flour 2 (9-inch) round cake pans. Sift flour, baking soda and salt into a medium-size bowl. In a large bowl, cream butter. Gradually add sugar and vanilla, beating until mixture is fluffy. Add eggs, 1 at a time, beating well after each addition. Blend in melted chocolate. Add dry ingredients alternately with ice water and food coloring. Mix batter 2 minutes or until well-blended. Pour into prepared pans. Bake in preheated oven 30 to 35 minutes or until a wooden pick inserted into center comes out clean. Cool in pans on a wire rack 10 minutes. Remove from pans; cool completely. Makes 1 (9-inch) 2-layer cake.

Helen Rushton   Greenfield, Indiana   Indiana State Fair

Devil's Food Loaf Cake

Fair time is popular with Terrill Lutes' children and colleagues at work, because they get to eat the experiments that didn't make it. But even better is being able to enjoy a cake like this one, which flaunts a blue ribbon. Entered in the unfrosted cake class, this dark, sweet, light-textured loaf cake would be complemented by Chocolate Whipped Cream Frosting, pages 70-71, or a bittersweet chocolate glaze.

2-1/4 cups all-purpose flour
1/2 cup unsweetened cocoa powder
1-1/2 teaspoons baking soda
1 teaspoon salt
1/2 cup shortening
1-3/4 cups sugar
1 teaspoon vanilla extract
3 eggs, separated
1-1/3 cups cold water

Preheat oven to 350F (175C). Generously grease and flour a 13" x 9" baking pan. In a medium-size bowl, mix flour, cocoa powder, baking soda and salt. In a large bowl, beat shortening with an electric mixer on medium speed 30 seconds. Add 1 cup of sugar and vanilla; beat until fluffy. Add egg yolks, 1 at a time, beating 1 minute after each addition. Add dry ingredients and water alternately, mixing on low speed after each addition until just combined. Clean beaters. In a small bowl, beat egg whites until soft peaks form. Gradually add remaining sugar, beating until stiff peaks form. By hand, gently fold egg white meringue into batter just until completely mixed. Spoon batter into prepared pan. Bake in preheated oven about 35 minutes or until a wooden pick inserted into center comes out clean. If cake is to be removed from pan, cool in pan on a wire rack 10 minutes. Remove from pan; cool completely. Makes 1 (13" x 9") cake.

Terrill Lutes   York, Nebraska   Nebraska State Fair

Banana Layer Cake

Many California home bakers combine an interest in fresh, nutritious food with their love of rich desserts by specializing in cakes made with fruit, vegetables and nuts. So it takes an extraordinary banana cake to achieve blue ribbon status at the Los Angeles County Fair. Janice Livelsberger's special occasion layer cake includes coconut and pecans with a creamy pecan filling. For eye appeal, she frosts the sides and a border around the top, leaving the coconut-studded center of the cake unfrosted.

3/4 cup shortening
1-1/2 cups sugar
2 eggs
1 teaspoon vanilla extract
1 cup mashed bananas
2 cups sifted all-purpose flour
1 teaspoon baking soda
1 teaspoon baking powder
1/2 teaspoon salt
1/2 cup buttermilk
1/2 cup chopped pecans
1 cup flaked coconut

Creamy Nut Filling:

1/2 cup sugar
2 tablespoons all-purpose flour
1/2 cup half and half
2 tablespoons butter or margarine
1/2 cup chopped pecans
1/4 teaspoon salt
1 teaspoon vanilla extract

White Snow Frosting:

1 egg white
1/4 cup shortening
1/4 cup butter or margarine
1/2 teaspoon coconut extract
1/2 teaspoon vanilla extract
2 cups sifted powdered sugar

Preheat oven to 375F (190C). Grease and flour 2 (9-inch) round cake pans. In a large bowl, cream shortening and sugar until light and fluffy. Add eggs and vanilla; beat 2 minutes with an electric mixer at medium speed. Add bananas; beat 2 minutes. Sift flour, baking soda, baking powder and salt into a medium-size bowl. Add dry ingredients alternately with buttermilk to creamed mixture, beating after each addition until well blended. Stir in pecans. Pour into prepared pans. Sprinkle 1/2 cup of coconut on each layer. Bake in preheated oven 25 to 30 minutes or until a wooden pick inserted into center comes out clean. Cool in pans on a wire rack 10 minutes. Remove from pans; cool on wire rack. Prepare Creamy Nut Filling and White Snow Frosting. Place 1 layer, coconut side down, on a serving plate; spread with filling. Top with second layer, coconut side up. Swirl frosting around sides and 1 inch around top edge, leaving center unfrosted. Makes 1 (9-inch) 2-layer cake.

Creamy Nut Filling:

In a heavy medium-size saucepan, combine sugar, flour, half and half and butter. Cook, stirring constantly, until thickened. Stir in pecans, salt and vanilla. Cool.

White Snow Frosting:

In a medium-size bowl, cream egg white, shortening, butter, coconut extract and vanilla with an electric mixer at medium speed. Gradually add powdered sugar, beating until light and fluffy.

Janice Livelsberger   Glendora, California   Los Angeles County Fair

Sourdough Carrot Cake

Anyone who makes sourdough bread will welcome this good tasting carrot cake recipe which incorporates sourdough starter. Ruth Belden won both a blue ribbon and an award for the best-of-all frosted cakes at the New Mexico State Fair with this hearty, moist cake. If you don't have starter on hand, make it at least two days in advance.

1 cup Sourdough Starter
1-1/2 cups vegetable oil
2 cups sugar
2 teaspoons vanilla extract
3 eggs
2/3 cup well-drained crushed pineapple
1-3/4 cups shredded carrots (about 5 medium-size)
1 cup chopped walnuts
2-1/2 cups all-purpose flour
1 teaspoon baking soda
1/2 teaspoon salt
1 tablespoon ground cinnamon
3/4 cup shredded coconut

Sourdough Starter:

2 cups all-purpose flour
3 tablespoons sugar
1 (1/4-oz.) package active dry yeast (about 1 tablespoon)
1/2 teaspoon salt, if desired
2 cups warm water

Cream Cheese Frosting:

1 (8-oz.) package cream cheese, room temperature
3 tablespoons butter
2 cups sifted powdered sugar
1 teaspoon vanilla extract
1 to 3 teaspoons milk, if needed

Prepare Sour Dough Starter at least 2 days before preparing cake. Preheat oven to 350F (175C). Generously grease and flour 3 (9-inch) round cake pans or a 13" x 9" baking pan. In a large bowl, beat Sourdough Starter, oil, sugar, and vanilla. Add eggs, 1 at a time, beating well after each addition. Stir in pineapple, carrots and walnuts. Add flour, baking soda, salt and cinnamon, mixing until well-blended. Stir in coconut. Pour into prepared pan or pans. Bake in preheated oven about 55 minutes for 13" x 9" pan or 40 minutes for 9-inch-round cake pans or until surface springs back when touched with fingers. Cool in pan on a wire rack 10 minutes. Remove from pan; cool to room temperature. Prepare Cream Cheese Frosting. Frost top of 13" x 9" cake. Or spread 1 (9-inch) layer with frosting. Place second layer on top. Frost top of cake. Makes 1 (13" x 9") cake or 1 (9-inch) 2-layer cake.

Sourdough Starter:

In a large bowl, beat flour, sugar, yeast, salt and water. Fermentation will dissolve small lumps. Cover bowl with a cloth. Let stand in a warm place, free from drafts, 2 to 3 days until it has a good sour smell. Refrigerate starter in a covered plastic pitcher or glass container with a lid. Use within 2 weeks. Bring starter to room temperature before using.

Cream Cheese Frosting:

In a medium-size bowl, beat cream cheese, butter and vanilla until light and fluffy. Gradually add powdered sugar, beating until smooth. If mixture is too thick to spread, add milk, a little at a time.

Ruth Belden   Albuquerque, New Mexico   New Mexico State Fair

Spicy Applesauce Bundt Cake

If you consider applesauce cake a homey, family dessert, Clara Hess' Bundt version shows it also can be a special occasion beauty. Filled with golden raisins and chopped pecans, this moist, spicy cake tastes even better the second day. It keeps well and needs no frosting.

3 cups all-purpose flour
2 teaspoons baking soda
1 teaspoon ground cinnamon
1 teaspoon allspice
1/2 teaspoon salt
1 cup butter or margarine, softened
1 cup firmly packed light-brown sugar
1 cup granulated sugar
1 egg
2 cups applesauce
1 cup golden raisins
1 cup chopped pecans
Powdered sugar

Preheat oven to 350F (175C). Generously grease and flour a 10-inch Bundt pan. In a medium-size bowl, mix flour, baking soda, spices and salt. In a large bowl, cream butter, brown and granulated sugars and egg until fluffy. Stir in applesauce alternately with dry ingredients until well-blended. Stir in raisins and pecans. Pour batter into prepared pan. Bake in preheated oven 65 to 70 minutes or until a wooden pick inserted into center comes out clean. Cool in pan on a wire rack 20 minutes. Invert on a serving plate; cool. Sprinkle with powdered sugar. Cover lightly and store at room temperature. Makes 1 (10-inch) Bundt cake.

TIP The full flavor of this cake develops if baked the day before serving.

Clara Hess   Columbus, Ohio   Ohio State Fair

Our Favorite Gingerbread

Some fairs judge gingerbread with quick breads, some as a loaf cake. Mary Ann Hildreth's light, tender version is definitely a dessert. Not too spicy, it is delicious slightly warm with whipped cream and moist enough to enjoy as a snack cake for several days.

1/2 cup butter
3/4 cup firmly packed light-brown sugar
1 egg, beaten
1/2 cup light molasses
1 cup milk
2-1/2 cups cake flour
1/2 teaspoons salt
1 teaspoon soda
1 teaspoon baking powder
1 teaspoon ground ginger
1 teaspoon ground cinnamon

Preheat oven to 375F (190C). Generously grease a 9-inch-square baking pan. In a medium-size bowl, cream butter and sugar until well blended. Add egg, molasses and milk; beat until well blended. Sift in flour, salt, soda, baking powder, ginger and cinnamon. Beat until mixed; batter may look slightly curdled. Pour into greased pan. Bake in preheated oven about 30 minutes or until a wooden pick inserted into center comes out clean. Serve slightly warm or at room temperature. Makes 1 (9-inch) square cake.

Mary Ann Hildreth   Fairborn, Ohio   Ohio State Fair

Coconut-Topped Oatmeal Microwave Cake

Carla Bouffard says entering fairs is her hobby, and she has a collection of 577 ribbons from fairs from Maine to Kansas to show for it. Although many of her earlier awards were for needlework, she has found her preserving and baking are attracting more attention—and awards. Kansas is one of a handful of state fairs to recognize the growing number of microwave users by adding microwave cakes to its cake category. This sweet, hearty snack cake is a winning choice for microwave cooks.

1 cup quick-cooking rolled oats
1-1/2 cups water
1-1/3 cups sifted all-purpose flour
1 teaspoon baking soda
1 teaspoon ground cinnamon
1/2 teaspoon salt
1/4 teaspoon ground nutmeg
1/2 cup butter or margarine
1 cup firmly packed brown sugar
1/2 cup granulated sugar
2 eggs
1-1/2 teaspoons vanilla extract

Coconut Caramel Topping:

1 cup flaked coconut
1/2 cup chopped walnuts
1/2 cup firmly packed brown sugar
1/2 cup milk
1/4 cup butter or margarine
Dash salt

Combine oats and water in a 1-1/2 quart glass casserole dish. Microwave on 100% (HIGH) 3 minutes or until mixture thickens, stirring after 2 minutes. Sift flour, baking soda, cinnamon, salt and nutmeg into a small bowl. In a medium-size bowl, cream butter, and sugars until light and fluffy. Add eggs, 1 at a time, beating well after each addition. Blend in vanilla. Stir oatmeal mixture into creamed mixture. Gradually add dry ingredients to creamed mixture, beating well after each addition. Pour into a 12" x 8" glass baking dish. Microwave on 100% (HIGH) 10 to 12 minutes or until a wooden pick inserted into center comes out clean, rotating dish 1/4 turn every 3 minutes. Cool on a wire rack. Prepare Coconut Caramel Topping. Spread topping over warm cake. Serve warm or at room temperature. Makes 1 (12" x 8") cake.

Coconut-Caramel Topping:

Combine coconut, walnuts, brown sugar, milk, butter and salt in a 1-quart glass casserole dish. Microwave on 100% (HIGH) 6 minutes or until mixture is thick and bubbly, stirring every 2 minutes.

Carla Bouffard   Salina, Kansas   Kansas State Fair

Orange-Lemon Chiffon Cake

When chiffon cakes became popular enough to be included as a state fair entry, they presented a classification problem. Although they resemble cakes made without shortening, like sponge cake, they contain oil, so must be judged with shortening cakes. New Mexico solved this problem by having a separate class for chiffon cakes, which attracts many of the best bakers. When Donna Morgan's Orange-Lemon Chiffon Cake received a gold rosette for the best of 14 classes of uniced cakes plus the purple rosette for the best of show, this veteran blue ribbon winner reached her 10-year goal. Her advice to other aspirants: have all ingredients and utensils set out in the order you'll use them, preheat the oven—and let the phone ring.

2-1/4 cups sifted cake flour
1-1/2 cups sugar
1 teaspoon salt
1 tablespoon baking powder
1/2 cup vegetable oil
6 egg yolks, room temperature
3/4 cup orange juice
2 tablespoons grated orange peel
1 teaspoon vanilla extract
1 teaspoon lemon juice
8 egg whites, room temperature
1/2 teaspoon cream of tartar

Preheat oven to 325F (165C). Sift flour, sugar, salt and baking powder into a medium-size bowl. Make a well in center. Add oil, egg yolks, orange juice and peel, vanilla and lemon juice. Beat until satiny smooth. In a large bowl, beat egg whites and cream of tartar until stiff peaks form. Whites should be stiffer than for angel food cake. Using a rubber spatula, gently fold egg whites, 1/4 at a time, into yolk batter just until blended. Pour into an ungreased 10-inch tube pan. Bake in preheated oven 55 minutes. Increase temperature to 350F (175C). Bake 10 minutes more or until cake is lightly browned and springs back when lightly touched. Invert pan on a bottle or funnel until cake is cold. Loosen edges with spatula and remove from pan. Makes 1 (10-inch) tube cake.

TIP It is important to use correct measurement of eggs in this recipe. If using eggs other than large eggs, measure 1 cup egg whites and 1/2 cup plus 1 tablespoon egg yolks. Separate eggs while cold; let stand until room temperature before mixing cake.

Donna M. Morgan   *Albuquerque, New Mexico*   New Mexico State Fair

Robert E. Lee Cake

Derrik Van de Zande entered one of his favorite cakes in the Los Angeles County Fair on a whim, using "Mom's secret recipe" from his family home in North Carolina. Said to be a favorite dessert of the great Civil War general, this version of Robert E. Lee Cake is composed of three sponge cake layers marinated in a mixture of sweetened orange and lemon juices, rather than a filled and frosted cake. Stored in the refrigerator, this very moist cake will stay fresh for days.

9 eggs, separated, room temperature
1-1/2 cups sugar
2 cups sifted all-purpose flour
1/2 teaspoon salt
1 tablespoon lemon juice
Grated peel 3 lemons and 6 oranges
1/2 cup lemon juice (about 3 to 4 lemons)
2 cups orange juice (about 6 to 8 oranges)
1-1/2 cups sugar
1-1/2 cups shredded coconut

Preheat oven to 350F (175C). Spray 3 (8-inch) round cake pans with vegetable cooking spray. In a large bowl, beat egg whites until they hold stiff but moist peaks. In a large bowl, beat egg yolks until lemon colored and very light. Slowly beat in 1-1/2 cups sugar. Fold in egg whites. Then gently fold in flour, salt and 1 tablespoon lemon juice, mixing only enough to blend in flour. Divide batter equally among prepared pans. Bake in preheated oven 35 to 45 minutes or until a wooden pick inserted into center comes out clean. In a medium-size bowl, combine citrus peels and juices, 1-1/2 cups sugar and 1 cup of coconut. Stir mixture occasionally to dissolve sugar. Remove cake layers from pans to trays or large baking pans. Spoon citrus mixture over tops of warm layers; cool. Stack layers on a serving plate. Let stand several hours before serving to allow cake to absorb liquid. To serve, sprinkle top with remaining 1/2 cup of coconut. Makes 1 (8-inch) 3-layer cake.

Derrik Van de Zande Pomona, California   Los Angeles County Fair

German Apple Cake

A quarter of a century ago Joyce Dubois brought her first exhibit, a decorated cake, to the state fair. Now she enters as many as 100 items in foods, crafts and sewing and continues to excell as a cake baker. Lightly-spiced German Apple Cake is loaded with chunks of chopped fresh apples and nuts. The delicious moist cake develops a macaroon-like top as it bakes. It needs no frosting but would be extra-good served with a scoop of vanilla ice cream.

2 eggs
1 cup vegetable oil
1 teaspoon vanilla extract
2 cups sugar
2 cups all-purpose flour
1 teaspoon baking soda
1/2 teaspoon salt
1 tablespoon ground cinnamon
4 cups finely chopped peeled apples
1 cup chopped walnuts

Preheat oven to 350F (175C). Grease a 13" x 9" baking pan. In a large bowl, beat eggs, oil and vanilla; gradually beat in sugar until mixture is thick and creamy. Sift flour, baking soda, salt and cinnamon into a medium-size bowl. Add dry ingredients to creamed mixture, stirring until well blended. Fold in apples and walnuts. Spoon into greased pan. Bake in preheated oven about 45 minutes or until cake has started to pull away from sides of pan and a wooden pick inserted into center comes out clean. Remove from oven and cool on a wire rack. Serve slightly warm or cool. Makes 1 (13" x 9") cake.

Joyce Dubois   Wolsey, South Dakota   South Dakota State Fair

Cola Cake

Southerners don't just drink cola; they cook and bake with it. This unusual regional dessert is a variation of the moist, rich Texas Sheet Cake. Although Timothy Platt was named sweepstakes winner in the youth division for his cake, it appeals as much to adults as to young people. Timothy is an athlete who learned to cook in a home economics class and from his mother.

1 cup margarine
2 tablespoons unsweetened cocoa powder
1 cup cola
2 cups all-purpose flour
2 cups sugar
1 teaspoon baking soda
1/4 teaspoon salt
1/2 cup buttermilk
2 eggs
1 teaspoon vanilla extract
1-1/2 cups miniature marshmallows

Cola Icing:

1/2 cup margarine
6 tablespoons cola
2 tablespoons unsweetened cocoa powder
1 (1-lb.) package powdered sugar
1 teaspoon vanilla extract
1 cup chopped nuts

Preheat oven to 350F (175C). Grease and flour a 13" x 9" baking pan. In a small saucepan, combine margarine, cocoa powder and cola. Bring to a boil and simmer just until margarine melts. Remove from heat. In a large bowl, mix flour, sugar, baking soda and salt. Pour hot cola mixture over dry ingredients. Add buttermilk, eggs, vanilla and marshmallows. Beat until batter is thoroughly blended; batter will be thin and marshmallows will float. Pour batter into prepared pan. Bake in preheated oven 30 to 35 minutes or until a wooden pick inserted into center comes out clean. Prepare Cola Icing. Spread warm icing over hot cake in pan. Cool on a wire rack before cutting. Makes 1 (13" x 9") cake.

Cola Icing:

In a medium-size saucepan, heat margarine, cola and cocoa powder just until margarine melts. Remove from heat. Mix in powdered sugar, vanilla and nuts, stirring until well-blended.

Timothy Platt   Kathleen, Florida   Florida State Fair

Chocolate Whipped Cream Cake

Whipping cream replaces shortening and liquid in this delicate party cake. Blanche Falk's chocolate variation of this heritage white cake, enhanced by fluffy Chocolate Whipped Cream Frosting, will please everyone who prefers less-sweet cake desserts. Although the mixing method is unusual for a shortening cake, the cake is not difficult to make.

2-1/2 cups cake flour
1-1/2 cups sugar
2-1/4 teaspoons baking powder
1/2 teaspoon salt
1-2/3 cups chilled whipping cream
3 eggs
1 teaspoon almond extract
3 (1-oz.) envelopes premelted unsweetened baking chocolate flavor
Sliced almonds, if desired

Chocolate Whipped Cream Frosting:

2 cups chilled whipping cream
1 cup chocolate flavored syrup, chilled
1 teaspoon vanilla extract

🎗 Preheat oven to 350F (175C). Grease and flour 2 (8- or 9-inch) round cake pans. Line pan bottoms with waxed paper; grease waxed paper. Sift flour, sugar, baking powder and salt into a medium-size bowl. In a large chilled bowl, beat whipping cream until soft peaks form. Without washing beaters, in a small bowl, beat eggs until thick and lemon colored. Using a whisk or rubber spatula, gently fold eggs, almond extract and chocolate into whipped cream. Fold in dry ingredients until batter is uniformly brown and flour is incorporated. Pour batter into prepared cake pans. Bake in preheated oven 30 to 35 minutes for 8-inch cake pans or 20 to 25 minutes for 9-inch layers or until a wooden pick inserted into center comes out clean. Cool on wire racks 10 minutes. Remove from pans; remove waxed paper. Cool completely on wire racks. Prepare Chocolate Whipped Cream Frosting. Spread 1 layer with 1/3 of frosting; place second layer on top. Swirl remaining frosting over sides and top of cake. To serve, garnish with almonds, if desired. Makes 1 (8- or 9-inch) 2-layer cake.

Chocolate Whipped Cream Frosting:

In a chilled medium-size bowl, combine whipping cream, syrup and vanilla. Beat until soft peaks form.

Blanche Falk   Louisville, Kentucky   Kentucky State Fair

Savarin Chantilly

A feast-day dessert in France, airy, yeast-leavened Savarin, baked in a ring mold, makes an impressive company cake anytime. Cecilia Mootz takes classes and reads cooking magazines to develop her gourmet cooking skills. Indiana fair judges agreed that her glazed Savarin decorated with almonds and candied fruit was worthy of a sweepstakes rosette in the foreign foods category. When serving her cake to guests, Cecilia Mootz fills the center of the ring with vanilla-flavored whipped cream.

1 (1/4-oz.) package active dry yeast (about 1 tablespoon)
1/4 cup warm water
1/2 cup milk
1/3 cup butter or margarine
1/4 cup sugar
1/2 teaspoon salt
2 cups sifted all-purpose flour
2 eggs
2 teaspoons vanilla extract
1 cup sugar
2 cups water
1/2 cup kirsch
1-1/4 cups apricot jam
Blanched almonds
Candied cherries
Citron

Cream Chantilly:

2 cups whipping cream
2 tablespoons powdered sugar
2 teaspoons vanilla extract

🎗 In a small bowl, dissolve yeast in water. In a small saucepan, cook milk, butter, 1/4 cup sugar and salt over medium heat, stirring until butter melts. Pour into a large bowl. Cool to lukewarm. Beat in softened yeast, 1/2 cup of flour and eggs. Add vanilla and remaining 1-1/2 cups of flour. Beat vigorously 5 to 7 minutes. Cover and let rise in a warm place 1 to 1-1/2 hours or until doubled in volume. Generously grease a 6-cup ring mold. Stir down batter; spoon into greased ring mold. Cover and let rise in a warm place about 45 minutes or until almost doubled in volume. Preheat oven to 375F (190C). Bake in preheated oven about 30 minutes or until deep golden brown and Savarin begins to shrink from side of mold. If it browns too fast, cover lightly with foil. While cake is baking, in a small saucepan, combine 1 cup of sugar and water. Bring to a boil; cook and stir about 1 minute or until sugar is dissolved. Remove from heat. Stir in kirsch; cool to lukewarm. Remove cake from oven; cool in pan on a wire rack 5 minutes. Remove from ring mold to a large pan or platter. Using a sharp knife, prick top of warm cake in several places. Slowly drizzle with lukewarm syrup. Let cake stand about 30 minutes, basting every few minutes, so it will absorb syrup and become soft and spongy. Cake can be refrigerated at this point and brought to room temperature before serving. To prepare glaze, in a small saucepan, heat jam to boiling. Remove from heat; force through a sieve to puree. Brush top of cake with warm glaze. Prepare nuts, candied cherries and citron as desired. Garnish with almonds, candied fruit and citron. Prepare Cream Chantilly. To serve, place Savarin on a serving plate. Fill center with Cream Chantilly. Makes 8 to 10 servings.

Cream Chantilly:

In a small bowl, beat whipping cream, powdered sugar and vanilla until well combined.

Cecilia A. Mootz   Indianapolis, Indiana   Indiana State Fair

Jelly Roll

Marjorie Johnson is a superb baker who has won many food company recipe contests as well as nearly 400 ribbons and nine sweepstakes awards in the 12 years she has been entering the Minnesota State Fair.

1 cup cake flour
1 teaspoon baking powder
1/4 teaspoon salt
3 eggs
1 cup superfine sugar
1/3 cup water
1 teaspoon vanilla extract
Powdered sugar
2/3 cup jelly, beaten slightly with a fork to soften

Preheat oven to 375F (190C). Grease a 15-1/2″ x 10-1/2″ x 1″ jelly-roll pan. Line with waxed paper. Sift cake flour, baking powder and salt into a medium-size bowl. In a small bowl, beat eggs using an electric mixer about 5 minutes or until thick and lemon colored; do not underbeat. Pour eggs into a large bowl. Gradually beat in superfine sugar; blend in water and vanilla on low speed. Gradually add dry ingredients, beating only until flour is incorporated and batter is smooth. After half a minute, stop beaters. Using a rubber spatula, check to see no flour particles remain on bottom of bowl or beater. Pour into prepared pan. Spread batter to corners, leaving batter just slightly thinner in center than at sides. Bake in preheated oven 12 to 15 minutes or until a wooden pick inserted into center comes out clean. Sprinkle a clean kitchen towel with powdered sugar. Loosen cake from edges of pan; invert on towel. Carefully remove waxed paper. Trim away crisp edges. Spread jelly evenly on cake; roll cake lengthwise. Cool, seam-side-down, on a wire rack. Sprinkle with powdered sugar. Makes 1 (15-inch) rolled cake.

Marjorie Johnson   Robbinsdale, Minnesota   Minnesota State Fair

What hymns are sung, what praises said
for home-made miracles of bread?
        Louis Untermeyer

Minnesota's all-time champion bread baker acknowledges that years ago she started exhibiting so she could learn from the judges' score cards what she needed to do to improve her yeast baking skills. Whether it is the urge to compete or the rare opportunity to get expert evaluation, an increasing number of women and men are entering their yeast baking at many of the state fairs. Minnesota judges have had to resort to using fractions of points to determine blue ribbon winners from the large number of entries in the highly-competitive white and whole-wheat bread categories.

At a time when food manufacturers are promoting methods and recipes to speed up the baking process, it is interesting to observe that virtually all the prize-winners use the most traditional methods. Most dissolve yeast in warm water rather than mixing it with other ingredients; three-rise breads are not uncommon, and most emphasize kneading the dough the maximum time. One winner even grinds his own whole-wheat flour. Obviously, when a blue ribbon is at stake, the best bread bakers believe you shouldn't hurry the process.

As a result, the quality of prize-winning recipes from the most competitive states is outstanding. They include bread, with an emphasis on whole grains, sweet and dinner rolls, and coffee cakes. Recipes range from ones a novice baker could easily make to a few that require more experience. All are recipes you will treasure. You may want to bake your way through the chapter.

All About Flour

Breads in this and the Quick Bread chapters call for the kind of flour in the winner's recipe. To substitute flour in any of the recipes, follow these guidelines:

All-Purpose Flour: Milled from a blend of high-protein, strong-gluten hard wheat and lower-protein soft wheat, it is suitable for all kinds of baking, from yeast breads to delicate quick coffee cakes. Unbleached and bleached all-purpose flour can be used interchangably. Unbleached has a slightly higher protein content, so some prefer it for yeast baking.

Yeast breads made with all-purpose flour do not require as much kneading as those made with bread flour. Usually the gluten will develop the elastic network that gives the bread its structure and the dough will become smooth and elastic with five to eight minutes of kneading. It is all right to knead a few minutes longer, but overkneading can produce large holes in the bread. Sacks of all-purpose flour with nutrition labeling will show 11 to 13 grams of protein per cup of flour.

Bread Flour: High-protein unbleached flour milled from hard wheat, bread flour has a small amount of malted barley flour, added to improve yeast activity, and potassium bromate, which acts as a dough conditioner. This makes it easier to develop the strong gluten when kneading by hand.

Because of the strong gluten, bread flour makes higher, lighter loaves than all-purpose flour. When used in combination with dark flours, it gives yeast breads a better gluten structure, higher volume and finer texture. Bread flour also helps free-form breads, which are not baked in loaf pans, retain their shape as they bake. If you substitute bread flour in a recipe calling for all-purpose flour, make these two changes: knead the dough for at least 10 minutes and let the dough rest, covered, 10 to 15 minutes before shaping the loaves or rolls.

The nutrition label on bread flour will show 14 grams of protein per cup of flour. Some regional brands of flour also are high-protein, strong-gluten flours. Those without the additives in bread flour make excellent yeast breads, but may be a little more difficult for inexperienced yeast bakers to use without a mixer with a dough hook.

High-protein flours can be used in yeast batter breads as well as those which are kneaded. For recipes where you do *not* want to develop the gluten, like quick breads and cakes, use all-purpose flour instead.

Self-Rising Flour: One of the first convenience mixes, self-rising flour is a combination of soft wheat flour, salt and leavening in proportions suitable for making biscuits. While it can be substituted for the all-purpose flour, salt and leavening in some other baking recipes, it is best to use it only where it is specified. National brands of self-rising flour have 9 to 10 grams of protein per cup.

Whole-Wheat Flour: In recipes where the wheaty flavor and coarser texture is suitable, whole-wheat or graham flour can be substituted for up to half of the all-purpose flour without making other changes in the recipe. Because whole-wheat flour contains the wheat germ, it becomes rancid quickly. Buy it in small quantities and freeze it or store it in an airtight container in a cool place. In warm, humid weather it should always be refrigerated or frozen. Bring the flour to room temperature before using it for baking.

Rye Flour: Heavier than whole-wheat or all-purpose flour, rye flour is a high-protein flour with a low-gluten content. Used alone or with a high proportion of rye to white flour, it makes a sticky dough that is difficult to knead.

Grocery stores usually carry medium rye. Specialty food stores are the best source for light or dark rye and pumpernickel flours. Since it does not keep as well as white flour, all rye flours should be stored in an airtight container in a cool place and refrigerated or frozen in hot, humid weather. Bring the flour to room temperature before using it for yeast baking.

Bran: Unprocessed or miller's bran is the outer layer of the wheat kernel. It adds flavor and texture to breads. All-Bran cereal is a different product. Both kinds of bran are specified in recipes in these bread chapters.

All flour will absorb or lose moisture depending on a number of factors such as the way it is stored, the humidity and the temperature. Because of this, most yeast bread recipes give a range in the amount of flour.

More experienced yeast bakers often are able to use less flour, especially when kneading dough. But contrary to what some believe, it is possible to use too little flour. As a result, the bread may be crumbly or dense and soggy, and free-form loaves will not hold their shape.

Too much flour will make bread heavier. If you use extra flour and don't mix it in thoroughly, the bread can be doughy or even have small lumps in it.

Loaf Pan Sizes

To say that loaf pans come in various sizes is like declaring that there are different colors of blue. In testing the capacity of three loaf pans, each marked 8-1/2" x 4-1/2", we found that it required from 5 to 7 cups of liquid to fill each to the top. One was medium-weight aluminum, another was glass and the third was a heavier aluminum nonstick pan. All were from well-known manufacturers. Add to this the current proliferation of dark metal pans, most marked 9" x 5", and the difficulty in specifying pan sizes in recipes is compounded.

Anyone who has baked enough to know the characteristics of their own pans will have little trouble deciding which pan to use for recipes in these bread chapters. But for less experienced bakers or someone planning to buy new loaf pans, here are guidelines:

If the recipe calls for:

8" x 4" or 9" x 5" loaf pan	Size of pan is not a critical factor. Pan can be anything in this range.
9" x 5" loaf pan	Larger loaf pan required. An 8-1/2" x 4-1/2" pan that holds 7 cups will work equally well, but one that holds 5 cups is too small.
8-1/2" x 4-1/2" loaf pan	Any pan marked this size would do. Bread baked in a 9" x 5" loaf pan will have a wide, flat shape.
7-1/2" x 3-1/2" loaf pan	This pan and the 6-1/2" x 4-1/2" loaf pan each hold about 3 cups of liquid. You can make two loaves this size from any recipe that can be baked in a 9" x 5" loaf pan.

For state fair exhibiting, when appearance is important, it is worth noting that the 9" x 5" pan produces a wider, lower loaf than an 8-1/2" x 4-1/2" inch pan. This shape is particularly suitable for country-style breads. The higher, narrower loaf, baked in the smaller pan, will give the impression of higher volume from the same amount of batter or dough.

Muffin Pans

Muffin cups are more standardized than loaf pans, measuring 2 or 2-1/2 inches across. Pans that make super-sized 3-inch muffins are available, but none of the blue ribbon recipes specifies this size.

You will get about half again as many muffins using the 2-inch size as the 2-1/2-inch cups. The larger size is a good choice for sweet yeast rolls.

Elaine Janas' Yeast Baking Tips

Minnesota's all-time yeast bread champion has spent a quarter of a century developing her skills as a master home baker. Her approach is both scientific and intuitive. For example, she always uses a thermometer to measure the temperature of the water when dissolving yeast and weighs the dough to make sure her loaves are uniform in size.

On the other hand, she has observed the individual processes with such sensitivity, she says she can tell when the risen bread is ready for the oven by lifting the pan. It feels lighter to her than when she put the dough into the pan. And from the smell of baking bread, she can tell if it was made with all-purpose flour or her favorite mixture of bread flour and all-purpose.

Here are her suggestions for blue ribbon results:

In state fair judging, flavor counts for the most points. No matter how perfectly-shaped your bread is, it won't score well if it tastes flat or yeasty. Her recipe uses more salt than many. She believes this enhances the flavor without making the bread taste salty. The kind of flour you use also affects flavor.

For white bread she uses half all-purpose flour and half bread flour. She discovered this combination turns out bread like she made years ago, when the large sacks were filled with a higher protein flour than the five-pound sacks. Bread flour makes her loaves high, light and adds flavor; all-purpose flour contributes fine, even grain.

Dough made with bread flour should be kneaded 10 minutes to develop the gluten. She considers that a minimum and usually kneads hers longer.

Also a blue ribbon winner in whole-wheat bread, she recommends buying new crop whole-wheat and rye flour in the late fall and freezing it for state fair baking.

An accurate thermometer that registers the low temperatures for the water used to dissolve yeast can be difficult to find. Elaine Janas depends on an unbreakable stainless steel thermometer used by professional photographers in the darkroom. She uses water at 110F (45C).

Make sure yeast is fresh by dissolving it with a little sugar in the water. Watch for it to foam up in about five minutes. She prefers regular active dry yeast, not the kind that makes bread rise faster.

Plastic wrap is the best covering to keep the dough and the loaves moist during proofing. If the surface of the dough dries out at any stage, the loaves will not be as attractive.

In addition, she prevents the loaves from drying out by lightly greasing the tops with shortening before the final proofing and brushing them with butter immediately after she takes them out of the oven.

Dividing the dough in loaf-sized pieces and letting them rest 15 minutes makes shaping easier. She forms the dough in oblongs to make shaping even quicker.

For evenly-sized loaves she weighs out 1-1/3 pounds of dough for each loaf. If there is dough left over, she makes a few rolls.

Air pockets in the dough cause holes in the baked loaves. To get the fairly fine, even texture judges look for, she rolls the dough in a rectangle about 18" x 9", then rolls the dough tight, starting at the short end.

Her state fair bread always can be identified by its high crown. To achieve this, she lets the bread rise almost as high as she wants it when baked.

What she spends on a yeast thermometer, she saves in baking pans. Her trusty, medium-weight seamless aluminum pans are 8-1/2" x 4-1/2". She bought them several years ago in a discount store and has never found anything she likes better.

Dakota Rye Bread

Louise Schneiderman's prize recipe calls for using molasses as the sweetener. This bread rises three times.

1 cup milk
2 teaspoons salt
3 tablespoons shortening
3 tablespoons molasses
1 (1/4-oz.) package active dry yeast (about 1 tablespoon) or 1 cake compressed yeast
1 cup warm water (110F/45C for dry yeast, 95F/35C for compressed yeast)
3-1/3 to 4-1/2 cups all-purpose flour
2 cups medium rye flour
1 egg white beaten with 1 tablespoon water

In a small saucepan, heat milk, salt, shortening and molasses until shortening melts. Pour into a large bowl and cool to lukewarm. Meanwhile, dissolve yeast in warm water. Add dissolved yeast and 2 cups of all-purpose flour to milk mixture. Blend at low speed with mixer until flour is moistened. Beat at medium speed 3 minutes. Stir in rye flour and work in additional all-purpose flour to make a stiff dough. Turn out dough onto a floured surface. Knead 5 minutes or until dough is smooth and elastic, adding a little more flour, if necessary. Wash and grease large bowl. Place dough in greased bowl, cover and let rise in a warm place until light and doubled in size, about 1 to 1-1/2 hours. Punch down dough; let rise again until doubled in size, about 1 hour. Punch down dough again. Divide dough in half; shape in balls. Turn out dough onto a lightly floured surface. Cover and let rest 15 minutes. Grease a baking sheet. Shape in 2 round loaves; place on greased baking sheet. Cover and let rise in a warm place until doubled in size. Preheat oven to 350F (175C). Brush egg white mixture over loaves. Bake in preheated oven 35 to 45 minutes or until loaves sound hollow when lightly tapped. Remove from baking sheet immediately; cool on wire racks. Makes 2 large round loaves.

Louise Schneiderman Bottineau, N. Dakota   N. Dakota State Fair

Sweepstakes White Bread

When an exhibitor wins a blue ribbon in the same "lot" three successive years at the Minnesota State Fair, she or he must skip two years before entering in the same classification again. So Minnesota home bakers now have two years to try for the top prize in white bread as Elaine Janas takes her brief hiatus. In a state where superb yeast bakers abound, the bread categories are so competitive that judges have to resort to using fractions of points to award ribbons. But Elaine Janas is the all-time champion, as her bread wins the sweepstakes award for the best-of-all bread entries, in addition to blue ribbons for white bread. Besides sharing her recipe here, she also offers some of her baking secrets that have never been published. See Elaine Janas' Yeast Baking Tips, pages 80-81. She credits state fair judges with helping her perfect her yeast baking as she studied score cards and made changes to improve her recipe and technique during the nearly 25 years since she entered her first loaf of bread. Her big three-rise recipe makes four loaves of bread.

2 (1/4-oz.) packages active dry yeast (5 teaspoons)
1/2 cup warm water (110F/45C)
1 teaspoon sugar
2 cups milk, scalded
1/3 cup sugar
1/3 cup shortening
2 tablespoons salt
1-1/2 cups cold water
5 to 5-1/2 cups all-purpose flour
5 to 5-1/2 cups bread flour
Butter

In a small bowl, dissolve yeast in warm water with 1 teaspoon sugar. In a large bowl, combine scalded milk, 1/3 cup sugar, shortening and salt. Add cold water to cool mixture to lukewarm. Stir in dissolved yeast, 2 cups of all-purpose flour and 2 cups of bread flour. Beat well, until smooth. By hand, stir in enough additional flour to form a stiff dough. Turn out dough onto a floured surface. Knead a minimum of 10 minutes or until dough is smooth and elastic. Wash and grease large bowl. Place dough in greased bowl. Cover with plastic film; let rise in a warm place, 1 to 1-1/4 hours or until doubled in size. Punch down dough. Cover; let rise 30 minutes. Punch down dough. Divide dough in 4 pieces; shape in oblongs. Cover with an inverted bowl and let rest 15 minutes. Grease 4 (8-1/2" x 4-1/2") loaf pans. Shape dough pieces in loaves. Place in greased pans and lightly grease tops of loaves. Cover and let rise until loaves are light and almost as high as you want them when baked, about 45 to 60 minutes. Preheat oven to 400F (205C). Bake in preheated oven 45 minutes or until loaves sound hollow when lightly tapped. Remove from pans. Immediately butter tops of warm loaves. Makes 4 loaves.

Elaine Janas   Minneapolis, Minnesota   Minnesota State Fair

Parmesan Cheese Bread

Dorothy Miller's cheese bread is such a favorite with her family that she has worked out herb-flavored and sweet bread variations. Pressed for time, she even makes it with thawed frozen bread dough. This original blue ribbon version also brought first place ratings to daughters Patty and Pamela in the junior fair division of the Los Angeles County Fair. Although the savory bread is shaped like a pull-apart bubble loaf, she bakes the cheese-topped balls in loaf pans, so the bread can be sliced. Because the heavy Parmesan coating can make the bread stick to the pan, bake it in greased nonstick pans. The flavor and texture of the bread are superb. Daughter Pamela says, "Practice is the secret to success in making this bread." You'll agree it is worth some effort to get a perfect loaf.

1 (1/4-oz.) package active dry yeast (about 1 tablespoon)
1/4 cup warm water (105/40C to 115F/45C)
3 tablespoons sugar
2 teaspoons salt
2 cups warm milk
2 tablespoons butter, melted
6 to 6-1/2 cups bread flour
1/2 cup butter, melted
1 cup Parmesan cheese

In a large bowl, soften yeast in warm water with 1 teaspoon of sugar. Let stand in a warm place until foamy, about 10 minutes. Add remaining sugar, salt, milk, 2 tablespoons melted butter and 3 cups of flour. Blend at low speed with mixer until flour is moistened, then beat at medium speed 3 minutes. Stir in enough additional flour until dough pulls away from sides of bowl. Turn out dough onto a floured surface. Knead 10 minutes or until dough is smooth and elastic, adding additional flour if necessary. Wash and grease large bowl.

Place dough in greased bowl, cover and let rise in a warm place 1 to 1-1/2 hours or until doubled in size. Punch down dough and let rise again until doubled in size, about 45 minutes. Generously grease a nonstick 8" x 5" or 9" x 5" loaf pan. Punch down dough. Divide in half. Cover second piece of dough with an inverted bowl while shaping first loaf. Shape dough in a ball; divide evenly in 12 pieces. Dip each piece into melted butter, then into cheese. In greased pan, arrange 8 balls of dough in 2 rows, forming 1 layer. Place remaining 4 balls of dough as a second layer down middle of pan. Form remaining dough in a second loaf. Pour any remaining butter over loaves and sprinkle with any extra cheese. Cover and let rise in a warm place until doubled in size. Preheat oven to 350F (175C). Bake in preheated oven about 30 minutes or until dark golden brown and loaves sound hollow when tapped. If bread is browning too quickly, cover with foil after 20 minutes. Carefully remove from pans. Cool on a wire rack. Makes 2 loaves.

TIP Substitute foil-lined glass or aluminum loaf pans if nonstick are not available. Grease foil well. Reduce temperature to 325F (165C) for glass pans. If bread is overbaked, it will be more difficult to remove from pans.

Dorothy Miller Riverside, California   Los Angeles County Fair

Southern Sourdough Bread

An unusual sourdough bread made with a starter that is kin to the "Herman" sweet cultured starter popular in the early 1980's won blue ribbons for bakers in two Southern states. Harriet Holley, a nurse who also occasionally works for a caterer, won first prize two successive years at the South Carolina fair. Ruth Ford, who also was awarded the baking sweepstakes at a regional fair in Florida as well as the blue ribbon at the state fair, says the bread improves as the starter ages. The bread is sweeter and more moist then traditional sourdough because the starter includes instant potato flakes and sugar. To compare starter recipes, see Sourdough Carrot Cake, page 58.

1 cup Sourdough Starter, room temperature
6 cups bread flour
2 teaspoons salt
1/3 cup sugar
1-1/3 cups warm water (105F/40C to 115F/45C)
1/2 cup corn oil
Butter

Sourdough Starter:
1 (1/4-oz.) package active dry yeast (about 1 tablespoon)
2-1/2 cups warm water (105F/40C to 115F/45C)
1 cup bread flour
2 cups instant potato flakes
1 teaspoon salt
1/2 cup sugar

Prepare Sourdough Starter at least 6 days before making bread. Mix flour, salt and sugar in a large bowl. Make a well in center and add starter, warm water and oil. Beat until well blended. Oil top of dough, cover with plastic wrap and let rise in a warm spot until tripled in bulk, 4 to 12 hours. Generously grease 3 (8" x 4" or 8-1/2" x 4-1/2") loaf pans. Punch down dough. Turn out dough onto a floured surface and knead 8 to 10 times. Divide dough in 3 pieces. Shape in loaves and place in greased pans. Oil tops of loaves, cover with plastic wrap and let rise in a warm place 5 to 6 hours, or until tripled in size. The small loaves may not fill pans. Bread will rise another inch in oven. Preheat oven to 350F (175C). Bake in preheated oven 30 to 40 minutes or until golden brown. Remove from oven and brush tops with butter. Remove from pans to a wire rack to cool. Freeze for longer storage. Makes 3 loaves.

Sourdough Starter:

In a large bowl, dissolve yeast in 1/2 cup of warm water. Stir in remaining 2 cups of warm water, flour, potato flakes, salt and sugar. Beat until smooth. Pour into a glass, plastic or ceramic container that will hold about 2 quarts. Let stand, uncovered, at warm room temperature 3 days, stirring mixture down several times a day. Cover container at night. Starter will rapidly increase in size as it begins to bubble and "work". It will have a strong yeasty smell. Cover and refrigerate 3 to 5 days, transfering starter to a smaller container, if desired. Makes about 2 cups.

To continue starter process, remove 1 cup starter for bread. Add 3/4 cup sugar, 3 tablespoons potato flakes and 1 cup warm water to remaining starter. Let stand at warm room temperature 8 to 12 hours, stirring occasionally, then refrigerate. Again you will have about 2 cups starter. To continue this process, use 1 cup of starter within 3 to 7 days and repeat feeding procedure for rest of starter. If not used within 7 days, give or throw away 1 cup of starter and feed remaining cupful. Starter works best in other sourdough recipes that call for some leavening, like pancakes or breads that use a combination of about 1 cup of starter and yeast.

TIP Dough also can be shaped in rolls or round or oblong loaves. Rising time varies markedly with this dough, but these shapes will triple in size somewhat faster than the loaves.

Ruth B. Ford   Montverde, Florida   Florida State Fair
Harriet Holley   W. Columbia, South Carolina   South Carolina State Fair

Deli-Pumpernickel Bread

With six hungry children who loved mom's homemade bread, Diane Tite wisely taught them and her husband how to bake with yeast. Now all eight Tites are state fair ribbon-winning bakers. She continues to enlarge her baking repertoire with challenging recipes like this superb dark rye bread. True bakery pumpernickel is almost impossible to duplicate at home, but this unusual combination of ingredients turns out an impressive substitute. Grated unsweetened chocolate helps give the traditional "black" color without adding discernable flavor. Potato flakes make the firm, crusty loaves more moist, so the bread keeps its good eating qualities longer.

2 (1/4-oz.) packages active dry yeast (5 teaspoons)
1/2 teaspoon sugar
1/2 cup warm water (105F/40C to 115F/45C)
2 cups rye flour
1/2 cup dry milk powder
1 cup instant potato flakes
2 cups All-Bran cereal
2 teaspoons salt
1 tablespoon caraway seed
1 tablespoon instant minced onion
2 teaspoons onion powder
2 cups water
1/4 cup vegetable oil
1/4 cup dark molasses
1 ounce unsweetened chocolate, grated
2 to 3 cups unbleached all-purpose flour
1/4 cup water
1/2 teaspoon cornstarch
2 teaspoons caraway seeds

In a small bowl, combine yeast, sugar and 1/2 cup warm water. Let stand until bubbly. In a large bowl, combine rye flour, dry milk powder, potato flakes, cereal, salt, caraway seeds, minced onion and onion powder. In a small saucepan, heat water, oil, molasses and chocolate just until warm. Stir into flour mixture with yeast. Beat until well blended. Add enough additional all-purpose flour to make a stiff dough. Turn out dough onto a floured surface. Knead 5 minutes or until smooth and elastic. Wash and grease large bowl. Place dough in greased bowl, cover and let rise in a warm place until doubled in size, 1 to 1-1/2 hours. Grease 2 (8-inch) round baking pans. Punch down dough; divide in half. On a lightly floured surface, shape each half in a round slightly flattened loaf. Place in greased pans. Cover and let rise in a warm place until light and almost doubled in size, about 35 to 45 minutes. Preheat oven to 350F (175C). Bake in preheated oven 40 minutes. Meanwhile, combine 1/4 cup water and 1/2 teaspoon corn-starch in a small saucepan; heat just to boiling, stirring constantly. Brush on loaves and sprinkle with caraway seeds. Bake 5 minutes more or until loaves sound hollow when tapped. Remove from pans. Cool on a wire rack. Makes 2 round loaves.

Diane L. Tite   St. Clair Shores, Michigan   Michigan State Fair

Danish Oat Bread

Linda Shaw has her roots firmly planted in California, where her family settled in the 1890's. She and her husband have a backyard orchard and raise blackberries and grapes. She turns these into prize winning jams and preserved fruit, but most of all she enjoys baking bread. She started her own yeast bread baking years ago to keep up with her growing children's big appetites. Now she shares extra loaves with her co-workers at California State Polytechnic University. Danish Oat Bread is a hearty dark oatmeal-topped bread with a fine, moist crumb and a delectable flavor from the combination of oats and molasses. Instead of shaping it into two good-sized loaves, she sometimes makes one lavish round or oval loaf. For a slightly different version, she substitutes a coarsely-milled multi-grain cereal for the rolled oats.

1 cup water
1 cup milk
1-3/4 cups regular or quick-cooking rolled oats
3 tablespoons butter or margarine
1/4 cup dark molasses
1-1/2 teaspoons salt
2 (1/4-oz.) packages active dry yeast (5 teaspoons)
1/2 cup warm water (105F/40C to 115F/45C)
2 eggs
5-1/2 to 6 cups bread flour
1 egg yolk beaten with 1 tablespoon water

In a small saucepan, heat water and milk just to boiling. Pour over 1-1/3 cups of rolled oats in a large bowl. Stir in butter, molasses and salt. Let stand 30 minutes or until lukewarm. In a small bowl mix yeast in warm water; let stand 5 minutes. Blend oats mixture, eggs, yeast and 2 cups of flour at low speed with mixer until flour is moistened; beat 3 minutes at medium speed. Stir in enough additional flour to make a stiff dough that pulls away from sides of bowl. Turn out dough onto a floured surface. Cover with an inverted bowl and let stand 15 minutes. Knead 10 minutes or until smooth and elastic, adding additional flour if needed. Wash and grease large bowl. Place dough in greased bowl; cover and let rise in a warm place until doubled in size, 1 to 1-1/2 hours. Generously grease a baking sheet or 2 (8-1/2" x 4-1/2" or 9" x 5") loaf pans. Punch down dough. Shape in 1 large round or oval loaf or 2 round loaves and place on prepared baking sheet. Or shape in 2 standard loaves and place in prepared loaf pans. Cover and let rise in a warm place until doubled in size, 45 to 60 minutes. Preheat oven to 375F (190C). Just before baking, brush top of loaves with egg yolk mixture and sprinkle with remaining rolled oats. Bake in preheated oven about 1 hour for large loaf or about 40 minutes for standard loaves or until loaves sound hollow when tapped. Remove from pan to a wire rack to cool. Makes 1 very large loaf or 2 standard loaves.

Linda G. Shaw   Upland, California   Los Angeles County Fair

Squaw Bread

Southern Californians searched for years for a Squaw Bread recipe similar to the popular loaves sold in bakeries and served in restaurants in that area. Marilyn Martell (Cookie Baking Advice, page 130) is credited with developing an authentic recipe which has been shared with Southern Californians through recipe request columns in the Los Angeles Times. Fortunately, another good cook and frequent fair ribbon winner, Mele Bond, won first prize on her loaf of this delicious multi-grain bread and can share the recipe with home bakers across the country. *Do not omit the raisins*. The raisin liquid is one of the "secret ingredients" that gives the bread its moist texture and wonderful flavor.

2 cups water
1/3 cup vegetable oil
1/2 cup honey
1/4 cup raisins
2 (1/4-oz.) packages active dry yeast (5 teaspoons)
1/4 cup warm water (105F/40C to 115F/45C)
1 tablespoon honey
About 2-1/2 cups unbleached all-purpose flour
3 cups whole-wheat flour
1-1/2 cups rye flour
1/2 cup nonfat dry milk powder
1-1/2 teaspoons salt
Cornmeal
Butter or margarine, melted

In a blender, combine 2 cups water, oil, 1/2 cup honey and raisins. Process to liquify. In a small bowl, soften yeast in 1/4 cup warm water with 1 tablespoon of honey. In a large bowl, combine 1 cup of unbleached flour, 2 cups of whole-wheat flour, 1 cup of rye flour, dry milk powder and salt. Add liquid mixture and yeast; beat at medium speed with mixer about 2 minutes. Gradually stir in remaining flour to make a soft dough that pulls away from sides of bowl. Turn out dough onto a floured surface. Knead until smooth and elastic, adding unbleached flour if needed. Wash and grease large bowl. Place dough in greased bowl, cover and let rise in a warm place until doubled in size, about 1 to 1-1/2 hours. Punch down dough. Divide dough in 4 pieces. Cover with an inverted bowl and let rest 10 mintues. Lightly grease 2 baking sheets; sprinkle with cornmeal. Shape dough pieces in 4 round loaves; place on prepared baking sheets. Cover and let rise in a warm place until doubled in size, 45 to 60 minutes. Preheat oven to 375F (190C). Bake in preheated oven about 35 minutes or until crust is browned. Makes 4 medium-size round loaves

VARIATION Marilyn Martell's original recipe called for 1/4 cup honey and 1/4 cup brown sugar in the liquid mixture and brown sugar instead of honey in the yeast mixture.

Mele Bond Upland, California   Los Angeles County Fair

Butterhorn Crescents

Twenty years ago Dot Elgin was chosen to be in a television commercial because of her baking awards at the Oregon State Fair. That was so exciting for the first-time exhibitor that she has been competing and winning ever since. Her rich crescent dinner roll recipe can be mixed one day and shaped and baked later. Less experienced yeast bakers will enjoy working with the easy-to-roll chilled dough.

> 1 (1/4-oz.) package active dry yeast (about 1 tablespoon)
> 1 cup warm water (105F/40C to 115F45C)
> 1/2 cup shortening
> 1/2 cup sugar
> 1 teaspoon salt
> 2 eggs, beaten
> 4 cups all-purpose flour

Soften yeast in 1/4 cup of warm water. In a large bowl, cream shortening, sugar and salt. Add eggs and beat until blended. Stir in softened yeast and remaining 3/4 cup warm water; gradually stir in flour to make a stiff dough. Turn out dough onto a lightly floured surface. Knead about 5 minutes or until smooth and elastic. Wash and grease large bowl. Place dough in greased bowl, cover and let rise in a warm place until doubled in size, about 1 to 1-1/2 hours. Punch down dough, cover bowl tightly with plastic wrap or foil and refrigerate overnight or up to 5 days. After 3 to 4 hours, punch down refrigerated dough again. If storing longer than 24 hours, punch down once a day after dough begins to rise again. Grease several baking sheets. Divide refrigerated dough in 3 pieces. On a lightly floured surface, roll each piece in a 12-inch circle. Cut each circle in 8 wedges. Roll up, starting with wide end, then curve ends toward each other to form a crescent shape. Place point-side down 2 inches apart on greased baking sheets. Cover; let rise in warm place until light and doubled in size, about 40 minutes. Preheat oven to 400F (205C). Bake in preheated oven about 15 minutes or until rolls are golden brown. Makes 24 rolls.

Dot Elgin Salem, Oregon   Oregon State Fair

Bran Rolls

A veteran yeast baker, Dorothy O'Connell learned to make bread as a child, became 4-H project leader in baking, and more recently used her skills to improve school lunches in the local school district as a food service employee. The rich dough is a joy to handle; this is an excellent recipe for a novice bread baker to try.

3/4 cup All-Bran cereal
1/2 cup sugar
1-1/2 teaspoons salt
1/2 cup margarine or vegetable oil
1/2 cup boiling water
1/2 cup warm water (105F/40C to 115F45C)
2 (1/4-oz.) packages active dry yeast (5 teaspoons)
1 egg, beaten
3-1/2 to 3-3/4 cups all-purpose flour
2 tablespoons butter, melted

Place cereal, sugar, salt and margarine in a small bowl. Add boiling water and stir to melt margarine; cool. In a large bowl, stir warm water and yeast until yeast is dissolved. Beat in lukewarm bran mixture, beaten egg and 1-1/2 cups of flour. Beat 3 minutes at medium speed with mixer. Stir in enough additional flour until dough pulls away from sides of bowl. Turn out dough onto a floured surface. Knead until smooth and elastic, about 10 minutes. Wash and grease large bowl. Place dough in greased bowl, cover and let rise in a warm place until doubled in size, about 1 hour. Grease a 13" x 9" baking pan. Punch down dough. Divide in half; form in 2 balls. Cover half of dough with an inverted bowl. Divide remaining dough in 12 equal pieces. Shape each piece in a smooth ball. Place in greased pan. Repeat with second ball of dough. Brush tops with melted butter. Cover and let rise in a warm place until doubled in size, about 1 hour. Preheat oven to 375F (190C). Bake in preheated oven 20 to 25 minutes or until deep golden brown. Remove immediately from pan and cool on wire racks. Makes 24 rolls.

Dorothy O'Connell   New Brighton, Minnesota   Minnesota State Fair

Two-Way Caramel-Pecan Coffee Rings or Rolls

With a prize-winning sweet dough recipe, a knowledgeable state fair winner like Joanne Larson wisely uses it in several ways. With the same basic ingredients she makes handsome coffee cakes or everyone's favorite caramel-pecan rolls. Both her coffee ring and her sticky buns were awarded blue ribbons.

1-1/2 cups milk, scalded
2 (1/4-oz.) packages active dry yeast (5 teaspoons)
1/2 cup warm water (105F/40C to 115F/45C)
1/2 cup sugar
1/2 cup butter
2 eggs
5 to 6 cups all-purpose flour
1-1/2 teaspoons salt
1 teaspoon ground cinnamon
1/2 cup sugar
1 (2-1/4 oz.) package chopped pecans (3/4 cup)
6 tablespoons soft butter

Caramel Topping:
2-1/4 cups light-brown sugar
1-1/4 cups butter
5 tablespoons white corn syrup

🎗 Cool scalded milk to lukewarm. In a small bowl, dissolve yeast in warm water with 1 teaspoon of sugar. In a large bowl, cream remaining sugar, butter and eggs. Add lukewarm milk, yeast, 2 cups of flour and salt. Beat at medium speed with mixer 3 minutes. Stir in enough additional flour until dough pulls away from sides of bowl. Turn out dough onto a floured surface. Knead dough 8 to 10 minutes or until smooth and elastic. Wash and grease large bowl. Place dough in greased bowl, cover and let rise until doubled in size, about 1 hour. To prepare filling, in a small bowl, combine cinnamon and 1/2 cup sugar. When dough has almost doubled in size, prepare Caramel Topping.

Let topping cool to warm.

To prepare *Caramel-Pecan Coffee Rings*: Grease 3 Bundt pans or tube pans. Pour equal amounts of warm topping into greased pans. Sprinkle chopped pecans over topping. Punch down dough. Divide in 3 pieces. On a lightly floured surface, roll 1 piece to a 12" x 10" rectangle. Spread with 2 tablespoons of soft butter and sprinkle with about 2-1/2 tablespoons of filling. Starting at 12-inch side, roll up tightly. Pinch edges to seal. Cut in 7 (1-1/2-inch) slices. Place rolls on top of topping. Repeat with remaining dough and filling. Cover pans, let rise in a warm place 45 to 60 minutes or until doubled in size. Coffee ring will not fill pan. If you can't bake 3 coffee rings at once, refrigerate 1 to retard rising time. Move it to a warm place when first coffee ring goes into oven. Preheat oven to 350F (175C). Bake in preheated oven about 30 minutes or until top is deep golden brown. Let coffee ring cool in pan 2 minutes; invert on a baking sheet or serving plate. Let stand 1 minute more; remove from pan. Makes 3 coffee rings.

To prepare *Caramel Pecan Rolls*: Grease 36 muffin cups or 2 (13" x 9") baking pans. Punch down dough and divide in 2 equal pieces. Divide warm topping evenly between greased muffin cups or baking pans. Sprinkle pecans over topping. Roll dough in an 18" x 15" rectangle. Spread with 3 tablespoons of butter and sprinkle with 1/4 cup of filling. Starting with 18-inch side, roll up tightly. Pinch edges to seal. Cut in 18 (1-inch) slices. Place in greased muffin cups or pan. Repeat with remaining dough and filling. Cover pans, let rise in a warm place 30 to 45 minutes or until doubled in size. Preheat oven to 350F (175C). Bake in preheated oven about 20 to 25 minutes or until deep golden brown. Cool rolls in pan 1 minute. Invert pans on a baking sheet or a wire rack set over waxed paper. Let stand 1 minute; remove baking pan. Makes 36 rolls.

Caramel Topping:

In a medium-size saucepan, heat brown sugar, butter and corn syrup just enough to melt sugar, stirring constantly. Remove from heat. This mixture thickens as it cools. Do not prepare too far ahead of shaping dough.

Joanne Larson   Columbia Heights, Minnesota   Minnesota State Fair

Butterscotch Crescent Rolls

Utah boasts of an unusually large number of excellent bread bakers. Heather Young, already a blue ribbon baker at 15, got her early start in 4-H. She also has won prizes for chiffon cakes and cookies. Her tender sweet rolls incorporate butterscotch pudding in the dough, adding a delicate brown sugar flavor and rich golden color to the filled crescent rolls. The large recipe makes 4 dozen rolls.

1 (3-1/2 oz.) package butterscotch
    pudding & pie filling mix (not instant)
3/4 cup undiluted evaporated milk
3/4 cup water
1/2 cup butter
2 (1/4-oz.) packages active dry yeast (5 teaspoons)
1/4 cup warm water (105F/40C to 115F/45C)
1 teaspoon sugar
2 eggs
2 teaspoons salt
5 to 6 cups all-purpose flour

Filling:

1/3 cup butter, melted
1 cup firmly packed brown sugar
1 tablespoon flour
1 cup flaked coconut
3/4 cup finely chopped pecans

Frosting:

1/2 cup firmly packed brown sugar
4 teaspoons butter
1/4 cup undiluted evaporated milk
2 cups powdered sugar

In a medium-size saucepan, prepare pudding mix according to package directions using evaporated milk and water as liquid. Pour pudding into a large bowl. Add butter. Cool to lukewarm. Meanwhile, in a small bowl, soften yeast in 1/4 cup warm water with 1 teaspoon sugar. Add softened yeast, eggs, salt and 2 cups of flour to lukewarm pudding mixture. Beat at low speed with mixer until moistened. Beat 3 minutes at medium speed. Gradually stir in enough additional flour until dough pulls away from sides of bowl. Turn out dough onto a floured surface. Knead about 5 minutes or until dough is smooth and elastic, adding flour if needed. Wash and grease large bowl. Place dough in greased bowl; cover and let rise in a warm place until doubled in size, about 1 hour. While dough is rising, prepare Filling. Grease several baking sheets. Punch down dough. Divide in 4 pieces. On a lightly floured surface, roll each piece in a 15-inch circle. Cut each circle in 12 wedges. Using 1 scant tablespoonful of filling for each roll, spread filling on wide half of each wedge, pressing filling lightly onto dough. Roll up, starting at wide end. Place point-side down 1 inch apart on greased baking sheets. As soon as 1 baking sheet is filled, cover. Let rise in warm place until light and doubled, 30 to 45 minutes, continuing to shape remaining rolls. Preheat oven to 375F (190C). Bake in preheated oven 12 to 15 minutes or until golden brown. While rolls are baking, prepare Frosting. Frost rolls while still warm. Cool and store in air-tight containers or freeze. Makes 48 crescent rolls.

Filling:

In a small bowl, combine all ingredients.

Frosting:

In a medium-size saucepan, combine brown sugar, butter and milk. Cook, stirring constantly, over medium heat. Bring to a boil; cook 1 minute. Cool to lukewarm and beat in powdered sugar.

TIP   Because of the large yield of the recipe, with one oven you may need to let the last pan of rolls rise in a cooler place for a longer time.

Heather Young   Price, Utah   Utah State Fair

Big Batch Cinnamon Rolls

Cinnamon rolls are Sherry Stroud's speciality. Her husband Dennis can't resist them. Co-workers rave about them. Friends hope to get them at Christmas. After they took first prize at the county fair, she decided to see how they rated at the big-time state fair, where she was thrilled to get another blue ribbon. Her big batch recipe makes three dozen large rolls, but they freeze well, even after they are frosted. One of her secrets is to spoon the thin lemon-flavored glaze over the rolls while they are warm, so some runs down into the cinnamon-sugar filling. This small change makes a surprising difference in the flavor of these wonderful sweet rolls.

2 (1/4-oz.) packages active dry yeast (5 teaspoons)
3 cups warm water (105F/40C to 115F/45C)
1/2 cup butter
1/4 cup shortening
3/4 cup sugar
2 teaspoons salt
2 eggs
10 to 12 cups all-purpose flour
9 tablespoons butter, softened
1-1/2 cups firmly packed brown sugar
6 to 9 teaspoons ground cinnamon
1-1/2 cups chopped walnuts

Glaze:

1-1/2 cups powdered sugar
2 to 3 teaspoons lemon juice
1/4 cup butter, melted
3 to 4 tablespoons undiluted evaporated milk or cream

In a large bowl, sprinkle yeast on warm water and stir to dissolve. In a small saucepan, melt butter and shortening; cool to lukewarm. Add butter and shortening, sugar, salt, eggs and 2 cups of flour to yeast mixture. Blend at low speed with mixer until flour is moistened; then beat 3 minutes at medium speed. Beat in 3 to 4 cups of flour, then stir in remaining flour with a wooden spoon until dough pulls away from sides of bowl. Turn out dough onto a floured surface. Knead 5 to 10 minutes or until dough is smooth and elastic, adding additional flour as necessary. Wash and grease large bowl. Place dough in greased bowl, cover and let rise in a warm place until light and doubled in size, about 1 to 1-1/2 hours. Butter 2 (13″ x 9″) baking pans. Punch down dough; divide dough in 3 pieces and shape in balls. Roll out 1 piece at a time. Cover remaining pieces with an inverted bowl. Roll 1 ball of dough in a 15″ x 7″ rectangle. Spread with 3 tablespoons of butter. Sprinkle with 1/2 cup of brown sugar, 2 to 3 teaspoons of cinnamon and 1/2 cup of nuts. Starting from long side, roll up, jelly-roll style. Pinch edges together to seal. Cut roll in 12 slices; place in buttered pans. Repeat with rest of dough and filling ingredients. Cover and let rise in a warm place until doubled in size. Preheat oven to 350F (175C). Bake in preheated oven 25 to 30 minutes or until golden brown. Turn rolls out on a wire rack; turn right-side-up on waxed paper or foil. Prepare Glaze. Spoon and spread glaze over rolls while they are still warm, letting it run down into rolls. Freeze rolls well wrapped in foil or sealed in plastic bags. Thaw in wrapping, then unwrap and heat for a few minutes in a 350F (175C) oven. Makes 36 rolls.

Glaze:

In a medium-size bowl, mix powdered sugar, 2 teaspoons of lemon juice, butter and enough milk to make a thin glaze. Stir in additional lemon juice, if desired.

Sherry Stroud   Woodland, California　　　　　　　　California State Fair

Frosted Orange Bowknots

Bonnie Lillemon grew up in a big farm family where all the baking, including bread and rolls, always was done at home. Later, with five sons to cook for, she had a strong incentive to continue her family tradition of keeping the cookie jar filled and baking yeast breads and rolls for family meals, although she worked as a registered nurse. Now retired, she has time to bake for fun, which includes exhibiting at the state fair. Her skill and experience is evident, as she has won prizes on every entry, nearly all blue ribbons. Her attractive glazed orange rolls include fresh orange juice and shredded peel in the batter. The delicate flavor is further enhanced by the orange frosting. Shaping the bowknots is surprisingly easy to do. It is a technique you might also use for dinner rolls.

1 cup milk
1 (1/4-oz.) package active dry yeast (about 1 tablespoon)
1/4 cup warm water (105F/40C to 115F/45C)
1/3 cup sugar
1/2 cup shortening
1 teaspoon salt
2 eggs, beaten
Grated peel 2 oranges
1/4 cup orange juice
5 to 6 cups all-purpose flour

Orange Frosting:

2 cups powdered sugar
2 tablespoons margarine, melted
3 to 4 tablespoons orange juice

In a small saucepan, heat milk to simmering. In a small bowl, soften yeast in warm water with 1 teaspoon of sugar. Place remaining sugar, shortening and salt in a large bowl. Add hot milk, stirring until shortening is melted. Cool to lukewarm. Add dissolved yeast, beaten eggs, orange peel and juice and 2 cups of flour. Blend at low speed with mixer until flour is moistened, then beat 3 minutes at medium speed. Stir in enough additional flour to make a soft dough that pulls away from sides of bowl. Turn out dough onto a floured surface. Knead 8 to 10 minutes or until dough is smooth and elastic, adding a little flour if needed. Wash and grease large bowl. Place dough in greased bowl, cover and let rise in a warm place until light and doubled in size, about 1 to 1-1/2 hours. Punch down dough. Divide dough in half and form in 2 balls. Place balls on a floured surface. Cover dough with an inverted bowl; let rest 15 minutes. Grease 2 baking sheets. Roll 1 ball of dough in a 10" x 8" rectangle. Cut in 12 (8-inch) strips. Roll each strip lightly under fingers in a pencil-like strand, tie loosely in a knot. Place 2 inches apart on 1 greased baking sheet. Repeat with second ball of dough. Cover; let rise in warm place until doubled in size, 45 to 60 minutes. Preheat oven to 400F (205C). Bake in preheated oven 10 to 12 minutes or just until light golden brown. These rolls will scorch on the bottom if overbaked. Immediately remove rolls to a wire rack to cool. Prepare Orange Frosting. Spread rolls with frosting. Makes 24 rolls.

Orange Frosting:

In a medium-size bowl, blend powdered sugar, margarine and enough orange juice until frosting is smooth and of spreading consistency.

VARIATION For a light glaze, use 1/2 of ingredients and drizzle over rolls before they are completely cool.

Bonnie Lillemon   Minot, North Dakota   North Dakota State Fair

Cherry-Pecan Coffee Ring

When Shirley Noltemeyer's children were old enough to learn how to cook, she wanted them to have a challenge. So she suggested that she and they each bake something to enter at the state fair. To their delight, each won at least one ribbon and exhibiting at the fair became an annual family event. One of Mrs. Noltemeyer's latest blue ribbon winners, Cherry-Pecan Coffee Ring, is surprisingly quick and easy to make. The rich dough isn't kneaded and only rises 20 minutes before it is shaped. The dough also is easy to roll out, making this rich, flaky coffee cake a good choice for a novice yeast baker who likes impressive results. This attractive yeast pastry is cut and shaped like a Swedish Tea Ring but has a bright cherry and pecan filling.

5 to 5-1/2 cups all-purpose flour
1/4 cup sugar
1 teaspoon salt
2 (1/4-oz.) packages active dry yeast (5 teaspoons)
1 cup milk
1/2 cup water
1 cup margarine
2 eggs, room temperature
2 cups chopped pecans
1 cup chopped maraschino cherries, well-drained
3 tablespoons sugar

Glaze:
1 cup powdered sugar
1/4 teaspoon almond extract
3/4 teaspoon vanilla extract
About 2 tablespoons hot water

In a large bowl, combine 2 cups of flour, 1/4 cup sugar, salt and yeast. In a medium-size saucepan, heat milk, water and margarine until very warm (120F/50C to 130F/55C). Margarine does not need to melt. Gradually add to dry ingredients and beat 2 minutes at medium speed with mixer, scraping bowl occasionally. Add eggs and 1/2 cup of flour and beat at high speed 2 minutes, scraping bowl occasionally. Stir in enough additional flour to make a stiff dough that pulls away from sides of bowl. Cover bowl with plastic wrap and a towel and let rise in a warm spot 20 minutes. Dough will not double in size. To make filling, in a small bowl, combine pecans, cherries and 3 tablespoons sugar. Grease 2 baking sheets. Turn out dough onto a well floured surface. Divide dough in half and knead each half a few times until smooth. Cover one ball of dough with an inverted bowl. Roll remaining half in a 14" x 10" rectangle. Spread evenly with 1/2 of filling. Roll up tightly, beginning at 14-inch side. Pinch seam to seal. Arrange dough on a greased baking sheet, sealed side down, in a ring. Pinch ends together. With scissors or a very sharp knife, make diagonal cuts 2/3 of way through at 1-inch intervals. Turn each section on its side, alternating left and right. Repeat with remaining dough. Cover and let rise in a warm place about 45 minutes or until doubled in size. Preheat oven to 350F (175C). Bake in preheated oven 25 to 30 minutes or until golden brown and crust looks flaky. Remove to a wire rack. Prepare Glaze. Drizzle on glaze while coffee cakes are slightly warm. Makes 2 large coffee rings.

Glaze:

In a medium-bowl, combine powdered sugar, almond extract, vanilla and enough hot water to make a smooth glaze.

Shirley Noltemeyer   Shepherdsville, Kentucky   Kentucky State Fair

Lawrence of Waldo Wheat Bread

You can duplicate the marvelous flavor of guidance counselor Larry Parker's bread made with home-ground whole wheat flour with wheat berries from a food co-op. Process a small amount at a time in a blender or food processor.

1 tablespoon fresh bulk yeast or 1 (1/4-oz.) package active dry yeast
1/4 cup warm water (105F/40C to ll5F/45C)
1 teaspoon sugar
1 cup milk
1/3 cup shortening
1/3 cup sugar
1 teaspoon salt
1 egg
1 cup coarsely milled whole-wheat flour
3-1/2 to 4 cups all-purpose flour

In a small bowl, dissolve yeast in warm water with 1 teaspoon of sugar. In a small saucepan, heat milk, shortening, sugar and salt until shortening melts. Pour into a large bowl and cool to lukewarm. Add yeast mixture, egg, whole-wheat flour and 1 cup of all-purpose flour. Beat at low speed with mixer until flour is moistened, then beat 3 minutes at medium speed. Gradually stir in all-purpose flour until dough pulls cleanly away from sides of bowl. Turn out dough onto a floured surface. Knead until smooth and elastic, about 10 minutes, adding additional flour if needed. Wash and grease large bowl. Place dough in greased bowl, cover and let rise in a warm place until doubled in size, 1 to 1-1/2 hours. Grease 2 (8-1/2" x 4-1/2") loaf pans. Punch down dough; divide in half. Shape in 2 loaves by rolling each dough half in a 14" x 7" rectangle. Roll up starting with shorter side. Place seam-side down in greased pans. Cover. Let rise at room temperature until doubled in size, 1 to 1-1/2 hours. Bread should rise about 1 inch above top of pans. Preheat oven to 350F (175C). Bake in preheated oven 30 to 35 minutes or until loaves sound hollow when lightly tapped. Makes 2 loaves.

Larry R. Parker   Kansas City, Missouri   Missouri State Fair

QUICK BREADS

One result of our increasing interest in health and fitness is that quick breads have been enjoying a resurgence in popularity. We can improvise by adding fruit, nuts, grated and pureed vegetables and whole grains to basic muffin and bread recipes, thereby increasing the nutritive value while creating delicious new flavors.

Besides substituting for yeast dinner breads or breakfast toast, these breads leavened with baking powder or baking soda are popular for snacks and even double as dessert. Many of the blue ribbon recipes reflect this trend toward making more nutritious breads while still retaining the qualities like fine texture, flavor and appearance necessary to win first place.

But the basics have not been forgotten: an authentic Southern biscuit recipe which includes expert tips for success is an example of quickly-made bread that is sure to become a family favorite.

Finally, for anyone who is more interested in challenging or unusual recipes, we tell you how to make prize-winning sour cream cake doughnuts and paper-thin Scandinavian flat bread baked on a grill.

Banana-Macadamia Nut Bread

While Kristyn Drews still lived in Des Moines, she and her mother, Judy Collins, had a friendly argument over who had the better banana bread recipe. Finally they decided to enter them both at the fair to let the judges decide. That year Kristyn's Banana-Macadamia Nut Bread brought home the blue ribbon, but the next year her mother was the winner. The quick breads are quite different; each will have strong advocates. Banana-Macadamia Nut Bread is a big light-colored loaf with a fine, even grain. The tropical flavor of bananas and macadamia nuts is a winning combination. Because all the ingredients are mixed in just 30 seconds with an electric mixer, it is quick to make.

2-1/2 cups cake flour or 2-1/4 cups all-purpose flour
1/2 cup granulated sugar
1/2 cup firmly packed brown sugar
3-1/2 teaspoons baking powder
1 teaspoon salt
1 teaspoon ground cinnamon
1-1/4 cups mashed ripe bananas
1/3 cup milk
1 teaspoon vinegar
3 tablespoons vegetable oil
1 egg
3/4 cup macadamia nuts, chopped

Preheat oven to 350F (175C). Generously grease a 9" x 5" loaf pan. In a large bowl, combine all ingredients except nuts. Beat at medium speed with a mixer 30 seconds or until dry ingredients are just moistened. Stir in nuts. Spoon into greased pan. Bake in preheated oven 60 to 70 minutes or until a wooden pick inserted into center comes out clean. Cool in pan on a wire rack 10 minutes. Remove from pan and cool completely on wire rack before slicing. Makes 1 loaf.

Kristyn L. Drews   Omaha, Nebraska   Iowa State Fair

Butterscotch Banana Bread

The luscious flavor combination of bananas, butterscot[ch,] spices and pecans puts Judy Collins' rich quick bread into the tea bread or light dessert category. Darker than most banana breads, the loaves may need to be covered with foil to keep from overbrowning in the oven. Because of the high sugar content from the added butterscotch morsels, the pans should be well greased and floured to keep the bread from sticking.

3-1/2 cups all-purpose flour
4 teaspoons baking soda
1 teaspoon ground cinnamon
1 teaspoon ground nutmeg
1 teaspoon salt
2 cups mashed ripe bananas
1-1/2 cups sugar
1/2 cup butter, melted
2 eggs
1/2 cup milk
2-2/3 cups chopped pecans
1 (12-oz.) package butterscotch morsels

Preheat oven to 350F (175C). Generously grease and flour 2 (8" x 4" or 9" x 5") loaf pans. In a small bowl, combine flour, baking soda, cinnamon, nutmeg and salt. In a large bowl, beat bananas, sugar, butter and eggs until mixture is creamy. Add flour mixture alternately with milk, beating only enough to blend. Stir in 2 cups of pecans and butterscotch morsels. Spoon batter into prepared pans. Sprinkle with remaining 2/3 cup of pecans. Bake in preheated oven about 60 minutes or until a wooden pick inserted into center comes out clean. Check after 35 to 40 minutes of baking. Cover tops with foil if loaves are browning too quickly. Cool in pan on a wire rack 15 minutes. Remove from pans and cool completely on wire rack before slicing. Makes 2 loaves.

Judy Collins   West Des Moines, Iowa   Iowa State Fair

Nut Bread

Marjorie Johnson writes comments on every recipe she tries, rating each from "wonderful" to "don't-ever-make-again." So when she reads a new recipe, she is able to compare ingredients and measurements with similar ones she already has made. Unlike many good cooks who constantly try out new recipes, she never throws the poor ones away but keeps them for comparison. This kind of systematic evaluation is one of the reasons she has been a sweepstakes winner 10 times in 12 years of state fair exhibiting. Her basic Nut Bread recipe, which rates "wonderful" with everyone who tastes it, is one of her sweepstakes awards. For fair exhibiting she baked it in two small pans, so she could see in advance how one looked after it was cut. Two of her tips for success are to line the bottoms of the pans with wax paper for easier removal and to let the batter rest 15 minutes before baking.

1/3 cup butter
3/4 cup sugar
2 eggs
3/4 cup buttermilk
2 cups all-purpose flour
1/2 teaspoon salt
1/2 teaspoon baking soda
1/2 teaspoon baking powder
1 cup chopped walnuts

Grease 2 (7-1/2" x 3-1/2") loaf pans. Line bottom of pans with waxed paper. In a large bowl, cream butter and sugar. Beat in eggs; blend in buttermilk. Sift flour, salt, baking powder and baking soda into a medium-size bowl. Stir dry ingredients into creamed mixture. Mix in walnuts. Pour batter into prepared pans. Let batter rest 15 minutes while preheating oven to 350F (175C). Bake in preheated oven 40 to 50 minutes or until tops are golden brown and a wooden pick inserted into center comes out clean. Cool 10 minutes; remove from pans and finish cooling. Makes 2 loaves.

Marjorie Johnson   Robbinsdale, Minnesota   Minnesota State Fair

Date & Walnut Bread

Nadine Blesener enjoys reading about food and subscribes to several magazines that specialize in advanced cooking techniques. She also takes international cooking classes. But for her winning state fair entry, she chose a classic American date nut bread. Her quick bread recipe, which makes two loaves, contains a lavish amount of fruit and walnuts. If you can resist tasting it right away, the bread will mellow and be easier to slice if you wrap it in foil and let stand overnight.

> 1-1/2 cups coarsely chopped dates
> 1/2 cup shortening
> 1-1/2 cups boiling water
> 4 eggs, beaten
> 1-1/2 teaspoons vanilla extract
> 2 cups sugar
> 3 cups all-purpose flour
> 3 teaspoons baking soda
> 1/2 teaspoon salt
> 2 cups chopped walnuts

In a large bowl, combine dates, shortening and water. Let stand 15 minutes or until mixture cools. Preheat oven to 325F (165C). Generously grease 2 (8-1/2" x 4-1/2") loaf pans. Beat eggs, vanilla and sugar into date mixture. Stir in flour, baking soda, salt and walnuts, mixing just enough to moisten dry ingredients. Spoon mixture into greased pans. Bake in preheated oven 60 minutes or until a wooden pick inserted into center comes out clean. Cool in pans on a wire rack 10 minutes. Remove from pan and finish cooling. For easiest slicing, wrap cooled loaves in foil and let stand overnight. Wrapped loaves will keep up to 1 week in refrigerator. Makes 2 loaves.

Nadine Blesener Minot, North Dakota   North Dakota State Fair

Chocolate Zucchini Bread

Zucchini bread for chocolate lovers is Margaret Long's appetizing solution for a new way to use the prolific vegetable. Just the thing to serve drop-in guests, the dark, moist quick bread also can double as a quick dessert accompanied by grapes or other fresh fruit. Either way, it's especially good spread with whipped cream cheese flavored with orange peel.

3 eggs
1-3/4 cups sugar
1 cup vegetable oil
2 ounces unsweetened chocolate, melted, cooled
1 teaspoon vanilla extract
2 cups finely shredded zucchini
3 cups all-purpose flour
1 teaspoon salt
1 teaspoon baking powder
1 teaspoon baking soda
1 tablespoon ground cinnamon
1 cup chopped nuts

Preheat oven to 350F (175C). Grease and flour 2 (9" x 5") loaf pans. In a large bowl, beat eggs until thick and lemon-colored, then beat in sugar and oil. Stir in chocolate, vanilla and zucchini. If zucchini is mature, drain grated zucchini before adding to batter. In a medium-size bowl, combine flour, salt, baking powder, baking soda and cinnamon. Stir dry ingredients into zucchini mixture just until well blended. Fold in nuts. Pour batter into prepared pans. Bake in preheated oven 50 to 60 minutes or until a wooden pick inserted into center comes out clean. Cool in pans 15 minutes. Remove from pans and cool completely on a wire rack before cutting. Wrap in foil and store in refrigerator or freeze. Serve at room temperature. Makes 2 loaves.

Margaret Long   Huron, South Dakota   South Dakota State Fair

Apricot-Almond Bread

Fruit and nut breads have always been popular in California, where many home owners look for ways to use crops from backyard trees. Debra Horst's attractive quick bread calls for three important California products—apricots, oranges and almonds. A delicious treat for breakfast, Apricot-Almond Bread also makes a nutritious snack spread with cream cheese.

1 egg
2/3 cup sugar
2 tablespoons vegetable oil
2 cups sifted all-purpose flour
2 teaspoons baking powder
1/2 teaspoon salt
1/4 teaspoon baking soda
1/2 cup orange juice
1/2 cup water
1 cup dried apricots, finely chopped
1 cup sliced almonds

Preheat oven to 350F (175C). Grease and flour bottom only of an 8" x 4" or 9" x 5" loaf pan. In a large bowl, beat egg, then beat in sugar and oil. In a medium-size bowl, combine flour, baking powder, salt and baking soda. Add dry ingredients alternately to sugar mixture with orange juice and water, beginning and ending with dry ingredients. Fold in apricots and nuts. Pour into prepared pan. Bake in preheated oven about 1 hour or until a wooden pick inserted into center comes out clean. Cool in pan on a wire rack 15 minutes. Remove from pan and cool completely before cutting. Wrap leftovers in foil and refrigerate up to 1 week. Makes 1 loaf.

Debra Horst   Lakewood, California   Los Angeles County Fair

Carrot-Walnut Muffins

Marjorie Faris considers herself first as a person who wins prizes for needlework. But when she wants to make up the 10 entries Michigan residents are allowed to enter at the state fair, she includes baking. The talented grandmother, who is also a musician and part-time secretary, knows how to make good pebbly-topped muffins that include nutritious ingredients. Chopped walnuts plus carrot chopped in the blender, rather then grated, give these delicious muffins a nice chunky texture.

1-1/2 cups all-purpose flour
1/2 cup sugar
2 teaspoons baking powder
1/2 teaspoon salt
1/2 teaspoon ground cinnamon
1/2 teaspoon ground nutmeg
1 cup chopped walnuts
1 cup finely chopped carrot (about 1 large carrot)
1/4 cup margarine, melted
1 egg
1/2 cup milk

Preheat oven to 400F (205C). Generously grease or coat 12 medium-size muffin cups with cooking spray. Sift flour, sugar, baking powder, salt, cinnamon and nutmeg into a large bowl. Toss walnuts and carrot with flour mixture. In a small bowl, using a fork, blend margarine, egg and milk. Add to dry ingredients, mixing with a spoon only until dry ingredients are moistened. Spoon into greased muffin cups, filling cups 3/4 full. Bake in preheated oven 20 to 25 minutes or until a wooden pick inserted into center of a muffin comes out clean. Makes 12 muffiins.

Marjorie Faris   Berkley, Michigan   Michigan State Fair

Date-Nut Refrigerator Bran Muffins

Anna Marie Davis' California version of refrigerator bran muffins adds chopped dates and nuts to the basic recipe. The batter for these nutritious muffins can be refrigerated up to one month. A senior engineer with the telephone company, she says her demanding job has taught her how to budget her time in the kitchen. Besides winning hundreds of state fair ribbons, she shares proper food preservation techniques as a volunteer Master Food Preserver through the California Cooperative Extension Service.

2 cups boiling water
6 cups All-Bran cereal
2-1/2 cups sugar
1 cup plus 2 tablespoons vegetable oil
4 eggs, beaten
4 cups buttermilk
5 cups all-purpose flour
5 teaspoons baking soda
1 teaspoon salt
2 cups chopped dates
2 cups chopped walnuts

In a medium-size bowl, pour boiling water over 2 cups of cereal; cool. In a large bowl, cream sugar, oil, eggs and buttermilk. Stir in remaining 4 cups of cereal. Sift flour, baking soda and salt into another medium-size bowl. Stir dry ingredients into creamed mixture. Fold in soaked cereal, dates and walnuts. Batter can be baked immediately or refrigerated in a tightly covered container up to 1 month. To bake, grease or coat medium-size muffins cups with cooking spray. Spoon batter into greased muffin cups. Let batter stand in muffin pans while oven is preheating to 375F (190C). Bake in preheated oven 20 to 25 minutes or until a wooden pick inserted into center of a muffin comes out clean. Makes about 60 muffins.

Anna Marie Davis Fair Oaks, California   California State Fair

Cranberry-Pecan Muffins

Now that Ruth Lundberg is retired, she has more time to bake for her grandchildren and her church and to cook for family gatherings of 100 or more. She began entering regional fair competitions nearly 40 years ago. After winning many ribbons and special awards, in 1986 she decided it finally was time to take on the big state fair. Acquiring 26 ribbons on her 38 entries, she will be a strong competitor on the state level. A generous amount of grated lemon peel adds a lively flavor to her blue ribbon Cranberry-Pecan Muffins. She keeps bags of the seasonal berries in the freezer, so she can make these attractive muffins any time.

1-1/2 cups coarsely chopped cranberries
1-1/4 cups sugar
3 cups sifted all-purpose flour
4-1/2 teaspoons baking powder
1/2 teaspoon salt
1/2 cup margarine
2 to 3 teaspoons grated lemon peel
2 eggs
1 cup milk
1 cup chopped pecans

Preheat oven to 400F (205C). Grease or coat 20 (2-1/2-inch) muffin cups with cooking spray. In a small bowl, combine cranberries and 1/4 cup of sugar. In a large bowl, mix remaining 1 cup of sugar, flour, baking powder and salt until well combined. Using a pastry blender or 2 knives, cut in margarine until mixture is crumbly. Add lemon peel. In a small bowl, beat eggs and milk; add to flour mixture, stirring only enough to moisten dry ingredients. Fold in cranberries and pecans. Spoon batter into greased muffin cups, filling 3/4 full. Bake in preheated oven about 20 minutes or until a wooden pick inserted into a muffin comes out clean and tops are lightly browned. Makes about 20 muffins.

Ruth Lundberg   Auburn, California   California State Fair

Double Good Buttermilk Biscuits

In the border state of Kentucky, biscuits are as likely to be made with all-purpose as self-rising flour. When Shirley Noltemeyer was first married, she spent four years trying out biscuit recipes and making changes until she had developed one she thought was just right. She prefers buttermilk for good flavor and tenderness and includes a little sugar. As a sweepstakes winner in breads at the Kentucky State Fair, her blue ribbon for biscuits contributed to her total score of the most points from ribbons on yeast and quick breads.

2 cups all-purpose flour
1 tablespoon baking powder
1/4 teaspoon baking soda
1/2 teaspoon salt
1 tablespoon sugar
1/3 cup shortening
1 cup buttermilk

Preheat oven to 450F (230C). Sift flour, baking powder, baking soda, salt and sugar into a medium-size bowl. Using a pastry blender or 2 knives, cut in shortening until mixture resembles coarse crumbs. Make a well; add buttermilk. Using a fork, stir quickly just until dough follows fork around bowl; dough should be soft. Turn out dough onto a lightly floured surface. Knead gently 10 to 12 times. Pat or roll dough 1/2-inch thick. Dip cutter into flour. Cut dough straight down; do not twist cutter. Place 1 inch apart on an ungreased baking sheet. Bake in preheated oven 12 to 15 minutes or until light golden brown. Makes 12 to 15 biscuits.

Shirley Noltemeyer Shepherdsville, Kentucky   Kentucky State Fair

Cinnamon-Apple Biscuits

As the wife of a U.S. Army chaplain, Tennessee native Elva Baldwin has lived in many areas in the South as well as New York and Germany. In each new post she has enjoyed learning about regional differences in food and collecting new recipes. Her biscuit recipe, which won the sweepstakes award, was a spur of the moment adaptation of her old favorite Southern "light" biscuits made with a low-gluten self-rising flour. Her comprehensive recipe demonstrates that she not only bakes great Southern-style biscuits, but she can turn a simple recipe into a lesson in making a blue ribbon product.

> 1/4 cup shortening
> 2 cups self-rising flour
> 1/3 cup finely grated peeled apple
> 1 teaspoon ground cinnamon
> 2 tablespoons sugar
> 2 tablespoons ground or grated pecans
> 1/2 to 2/3 cup milk

Preheat oven to 475F (245C). In a large bowl, using a pastry blender or 2 knives, cut shortening into flour until mixture resembles coarse crumbs. Do not overblend; overblending fat produces a mealy, rather than flaky tender biscuit. Mix in apple, cinnamon, sugar and pecans. Gently push mixture to edges of bowl, making a well in center. Using a fork, blend in just enough milk so dough pulls away from sides of bowl. Too much milk makes dough hard to handle; too little makes dry biscuits. Do not overmix. Turn out dough onto a lightly floured surface. Knead gently 10 to 12 times to develop structure and distribute moisture so biscuits will be flaky. Pat or roll dough 1/2 inch thick. Cut with a 1-1/2-inch biscuit cutter, dipping cutter into flour between cuts. Press cutter straight down without twisting to get well-shaped straight-sided biscuits. Or for more traditional-size biscuits, roll dough about 5/8-inch thick and cut with a 2- or 2-1/2-inch cutter. Push together remaining dough and reroll or pat out. *For crusty sides* place biscuits at least 1 inch apart on an ungreased baking sheet. *For soft-sided biscuits*, arrange with sides just touching in an 11" x 7-1/2" ungreased biscuit pan. Bake in preheated oven 5 to 7 minutes or until golden for 1-1/2-inch biscuits or 6 to 8 minutes or until golden for larger biscuits. Makes 15 to 18 biscuits.

TIP True Southern-style biscuits require self-rising flour, which is milled from soft wheat and is formulated especially for making biscuits. If self-rising flour is not available, substitute 1 cup cake flour, 1 cup all-purpose flour, 1/2 teaspoon salt and 2 teaspoons baking powder blended together for 2 cups self-rising flour.

Elva Baldwin   Columbia, South Carolina   South Carolina State Fair

Ohio Cornbread

A registered nurse who works full time and likes recipes that are quick and simple, Dorothy McGrath has won a number of special awards in the four years she has exhibited at the state fair. Her cornbread is the kind that Midwesterners consider the perfect version. Slightly sweet and finer-textured than many Southern and New England recipes. it is always made with yellow cornmeal and best served warm.

1 cup all-purpose flour
1 cup yellow cornmeal
1/4 cup sugar
4 teaspoons baking powder
3/4 teaspoon salt
2 eggs, slightly beaten
1 cup milk
1/4 cup margarine, melted

Preheat oven to 425F (220C). Generously grease a 9-inch-square baking pan. In a medium-size bowl, combine flour, cornmeal, sugar, baking powder and salt. Add eggs, milk and margarine. Mix only until well blended. Pour batter into greased pan. Bake in preheated oven 20 to 25 minutes or until a wooden pick inserted into center comes out clean and top is lightly browned. Serve warm. Makes 9 to 12 servings.

Dorothy McGrath   Hilliard, Ohio   Ohio State Fair

North Carolina Cornbread

Cynthia Weakley is a food service baker who thought her quantity recipe for cornbread was especially good. She adapted it to a home-size recipe and entered it at the state fair. Judges confirmed that she had a blue ribbon recipe. Southern cornbread recipes have many variations. Some use only cornmeal, no flour; many have little or no sugar. White and yellow cornmeal each has strong advocates, as do buttermilk or sweet milk. Thinner and less sweet than Ohio Cornbread, opposite page, this middle-of-the-road version of a Southern recipe has a delicious cornmeal flavor. As a tribute to its food service origins, it tastes as good at room temperature as warm from the oven.

1-3/4 cups all-purpose flour
1-1/2 cups cornmeal
2 tablespoons nonfat dry milk powder
3 tablespoons sugar
4 teaspoons baking powder
3/4 teaspoon salt
2 eggs, slightly beaten
1-1/2 cups water
6 tablespoons vegetable oil

Preheat oven to 400F (205C). Generously grease 2 (9-inch) round baking pans. In a large bowl, combine flour, cornmeal, dry milk powder, sugar, baking powder and salt. Add eggs, water and oil; stir just until dry ingredients are moistened. Pour batter evenly into greased pans. Bake in preheated oven 20 to 25 minutes or until a wooden pick inserted into center comes out clean and edges are brown. Makes 12 servings.

Cynthia Weakley   Raleigh, North Carolina   North Carolina State Fair

Hobo Bread

Because Jan Wagner's husband has to limit his intake of cholesterol, she welcomes recipes for breads made without eggs. Hobo Bread resembles a rich, sweet brown bread, baked rather than steamed. The raisins soak in boiling water with baking soda overnight or for at least 8 hours. Raisin liquid adds extra flavor and gives the bread its dark brown color. Baking the quick bread in coffee cans gives the loaves an unusual, attractive shape. As an extra benefit, you can store or freeze the extra loaves in clean cans sealed with their plastic lids.

> *2 cups raisins*
> *4 cups boiling water*
> *4 teaspoons baking soda*
> *2 cups sugar*
> *1 teaspoon salt, if desired*
> *1/4 cup vegetable oil*
> *4 cups all-purpose flour*
> *1 cup chopped walnuts*

In a large bowl, combine raisins, water and baking soda. Cover with waxed paper and let stand at room temperature at least 8 hours or overnight. Preheat oven to 325F (165C). Generously grease and flour 3 (1-pound) coffee cans. Combine sugar, salt, if desired, oil, flour and walnuts with raisins and liquid. Stir just enough to moisten flour and to make a stiff batter. Spoon into prepared coffee cans, filling each 1/2 full. Bake in preheated oven about 70 minutes or until browned and a wooden pick inserted into center comes out clean. Cool loaves in cans 5 minutes. Carefully remove from cans and finish cooling upright on a wire rack. Serve warm or at room temperature. Store in refrigerator or freeze in clean cans sealed with plastic lids. Makes 3 loaves.

TIP   Hobo Bread also can be baked in 3 (8" x 4") loaf pans. Grease and flour pans and bake 50 to 60 minutes or until a wooden pick inserted into center comes out clean.

Jan Wagner   Salem, Oregon   Oregon State Fair

Cheddar-Parmesan Cheese Bread

California youngsters can learn to improve their cooking skills as soon as they are old enough to start school by entering the Los Angeles County Junior Fair. Sarah LaPresle, who baked her first loaf of yeast bread when she was eight, gained valuable experience and a number of ribbons competing against her young peers. Now exhibiting with women who have been cooking for many years, she is still creating blue ribbon breads. Her savory cheese quick bread gets its authoritative flavor from the baked-on onion and cheese topping.

2 cups all-purpose flour
1 tablespoon sugar
1 tablespoon baking powder
1/2 teaspoon salt
1 teaspoon dry mustard
1/4 cup butter
1 cup (4 oz.) shredded Cheddar cheese
2 tablespoons grated Parmesan cheese
1 cup milk
1 egg
1/2 cup finely chopped onion
1 teaspoon paprika

Preheat oven to 350F (175C). Grease a 9" x 5" loaf pan. In a large bowl, combine flour, sugar, baking powder, salt and mustard. Using a pastry blender or 2 knives, cut in butter until mixture resembles coarse meal. Stir in 1/2 cup of Cheddar cheese and Parmesan cheese. In a small bowl, beat milk and egg just until well blended. Add to flour mixture and mix with a fork just until dry ingredients are moistened. Spoon batter into greased pan. In a small bowl, toss remaining 1/2 cup Cheddar cheese, onion and paprika. Sprinkle over batter. Bake in preheated oven about 60 minutes or until a wooden pick inserted into center comes out clean. Cool in pan on a wire rack 10 minutes. Remove from pan. Serve slightly warm or at room temperature. Or wrap in foil and refrigerate up to several days. Makes 1 loaf.

Sarah LaPresle Glendora, California   Los Angeles County Fair

Dutch Apple Coffee Cake

State fair time in Wisconsin also marks the beginning of the apple harvest. With baskets of excellent northern varieties for sale at every roadside market, Wisconsin cooks welcome recipes to use the abundant supply of fresh fruit. Beth Taticek's attractive quick coffee cake topped with a lavish layer of apple wedges is perfect to serve for brunch or for morning coffee. For best flavor and appearance use slightly tart cooking apples that keep their shape.

> 1/4 cup butter, room temperature
> 3/4 cup sugar
> 1 egg
> 1-1/2 cups all-purpose flour
> 2 teaspoons baking powder
> 1/2 teaspoon salt
> 1/2 cup milk
> 3 large or 4 medium-size cooking apples
> 1/4 cup sugar
> 1/4 teaspoon ground cinnamon

Preheat oven to 375F (190C). Grease and flour a 9-inch-square pan. In a large bowl, beat butter, 3/4 cup sugar and egg until well blended. Sift flour, baking powder and salt into a small bowl. Add dry ingredients alternately with milk to creamed mixture, stirring just enough to blend well. Spread in prepared pan. Peel and core apples; cut in 1/2-inch wedges. Arrange in slightly overlapping rows on top of batter. In a small bowl, combine 1/4 cup sugar and cinnamon. Sprinkle over coffee cake. Bake in preheated oven 30 to 35 minutes or until a wooden pick inserted into center comes out clean. Serve warm or at room temperature. Makes 9 to 12 servings.

TIP For her prize-winning coffee cake, Beth Taticek arranged her apple wedges in an overlapping brick formation, rather than in rows. If apples are especially tart, increase sugar to 6 tablespoons and ground cinnamon to a scant 1/2 teaspoon to sprinkle over coffee cake.

Beth Taticek   Delafield, Wisconsin   Wisconsin State Fair

Spicy Nuts Coffee Cake

Linda Ann Schofield is a high school library media specialist and a farm wife with five children. Her Spicy Nuts Coffee Cake has a crunchy streusel layer of nuts and brown sugar in the middle instead of sprinkled on top. This quick coffee cake not only is particularly good tasting, but it is much neater to eat than a streusel-topped cake.

1 cup firmly packed brown sugar
1/4 cup all-purpose flour
4 teaspoons ground cinnamon
1/4 cup butter, melted
1 cup chopped walnuts
3 cups sifted all-purpose flour
1 cup granulated sugar
4 teaspoons baking powder
1 teaspoon salt
1/2 cup butter
2 eggs, beaten
1 cup milk

Preheat oven to 375F (190C). Grease and flour a 13″ x 9″ baking pan. In a small bowl, combine brown sugar, 1/4 cup flour, cinnamon and 1/4 cup butter. Mix in walnuts. In a large bowl, combine 3 cups flour, granulated sugar, baking powder and salt. Using a pastry blender or 2 knives, cut in 1/2 cup butter until mixture resembles coarse crumbs. In a small bowl, blend eggs and milk. Add to flour mixture, stirring just until dry ingredients are moistened. Spoon a little less than 1/2 of batter over bottom of prepared pan to make a thin layer. Sprinkle nut mixture evenly over batter. Spoon remaining batter over nut mixture, gently spreading to cover; batter may not completely cover nut layer. Bake in preheated oven 20 to 25 minutes or until top is golden and a wooden pick inserted into center comes out clean. Makes 12 to 16 servings.

Linda Ann Schofield   Zanesfield, Ohio   Ohio State Fair

Flatbread

Many Scandinavians living in North Dakota are only one or two generations removed from their European roots, so it is not surprising that their state fair has a special entry classification for traditional Scandinavian pastries and breads. Family recipes for the cookie-like krumkaka and fattigman and the thin flat breads baked on a griddle like Norwegian potato lefse and Swedish flatbread often are closely guarded. Louise Schneiderman, an expert at making griddle breads, was willing to share her 50-year-old blue ribbon recipe, which originally came from an old state farm magazine. Flatbread recipes vary widely. Hers is unusual because it uses corn syrup instead of sugar and cream as shortening as well as part of the liquid. While many who bake lefse or flatbread regularly own a large round electric grill made especially for this purpose, you can bake the flatbread in an electric fry pan if you roll out smaller pieces of dough. The thin crisp rounds are served as a dinner bread in Scandinavian homes. They also can be eaten like an oversize-cracker with soup or served with cheese as an appetizer.

1 cup graham or whole-wheat flour
2-1/2 to 3 cups all-purpose flour
1 teaspoon baking soda
1/4 teaspoon salt
1 cup buttermilk
1/2 cup whipping cream
1/2 cup light corn syrup

🎀 Preheat electric griddle or frypan to 350F (175C). In a large bowl, combine whole-wheat flour, 1-1/2 cups of all-purpose flour, baking soda and salt. Add buttermilk, cream and corn syrup. Stir to make a smooth dough. Using a spoon or your hands, work in enough additional flour to make a stiff dough. Using 1/4 cup of dough for each flatbread, knead ball of dough a few times on a well-floured surface. Pat in a circle. Using a floured rolling pin, roll out in a paper-thin circle 10 inches in diameter. To prevent sticking, flip dough over several times during early stage of rolling. Make sure surface always is evenly floured or rolled-out flatbread will be difficult to remove. Wrap flatbread over a rolling pin or lift with a lefse turner or other thin flat strip of wood. Carefully transfer to preheated griddle or frypan. If surface bubbles, prick with a fork. Cook about 1-1/2 minutes or until lightly browned. Turn with a spatula and brown other side. Wipe griddle with a paper towel between breads to remove flour. Repeat with remaining dough. Preheat oven to 250F (120C). Place baked flatbreads on baking sheets. Bake in preheated oven 15 to 30 minutes or until dried out. Remove breads as edges become crisp. Store in a loosely covered container up to several weeks. Makes 10 to 12 large flatbreads.

TIP   To bake in a small electric fry pan, use 1-inch pieces of dough rolled to 4 to 5 inches in diameter. Makes about 9 dozen flatbreads. Flatbread also can be baked on greased baking sheets in a 350F (175C) oven about 15 minutes or until lightly browned.

Louise Schneiderman   Bottineau, N. Dakota   N. Dakota State Fair

Old-Fashioned Sour Cream Doughnuts

Using a sour cream doughnut recipe that had come from her grandmother, Rhoda McLain won a blue ribbon the first time she exhibited at the North Dakota fair. She has made these doughnuts so many times she says she no longer measures the flour but keeps adding until the dough feels right.

> 1 cup sugar
> 3 eggs
> 1-1/2 teaspoons vanilla extract
> 1/2 cup sour cream
> 1 cup buttermilk
> 4-1/2 to 5 cups all-purpose flour
> 2 teaspoons baking powder
> 1 teaspoon baking soda
> 1/4 teaspoon salt
> 1/2 teaspoon ground nutmeg
> Vegetable oil for frying

In a large bowl, beat sugar and eggs. Stir in vanilla, sour cream and buttermilk. In another large bowl, combine 4 cups of flour, baking powder, baking soda, salt and nutmeg. Add to creamed mixture, stirring just enough to moisten flour. Stir in enough additional flour to make a stiff dough. If desired, cover dough and chill for easier handling. When ready to shape, divide dough in half and refrigerate 1 half. On a floured surface, toss dough lightly until no longer sticky. Roll out to 3/8 inch thick and cut with a floured doughnut cutter. Reroll scraps and cut. In an electric skillet, Dutch oven or large saucepan, heat 2 to 3 inches of vegetable oil to 375F (190C). Using a pancake turner, slip 2 to 3 doughnuts into hot fat. Fry 1 to 1-1/2 minutes on each side or until deep golden brown. Using a slotted spoon, lift from oil and drain on paper towels. Roll, cut and fry remaining dough. Makes about 30 doughnuts plus holes.

Rhoda McLain   Berthold, North Dakota   North Dakota State Fair

SPECIAL COOKIES

I s there anyone who doesn't like cookies? And nothing can match ones baked at home. Whether it is a family favorite like oatmeal cookies or a festive confection baked only for the holidays, eyes light up when cookies come out of the oven.

State fair competitions provide an opportunity to see cookie making at its best. Entries run the gamut from plain to fancy. Since the "plain" peanut butter or molasses cookie that is awarded the blue ribbon may have won over dozens of other peanut butter or molasses cookies, all made by expert bakers, any cookie enthusiast knows those winning recipes are ones to treasure.

If you are looking for something more unusual—an international speciality like rosettes, a rich bar or an elegant little sweet to serve at a tea—you'll also find a good selection of those recipes here.

In addition to sharing their recipes, these prize winning cooks have divulged their secrets of success that make the difference between a cookie that is good or one that is best-ever.

Cookie Baking Advice from a Many-Time Winner

In addition to winning hundreds of ribbons for baked goods, cookie expert Marilyn Martell of Reedley, California conducts seminars and demonstrations on cookie baking and teaches adult education classes. Her tips for baking cookies that will please judges are:

Use the best quality ingredients.

Premeasure all ingredients before starting.

For tender cookies, mix just enough to combine ingredients well after adding flour. Overmixing will develop the gluten in flour and toughen the cookies.

For even-size cookies, use a level measuring tablespoonful of dough rather than a heaping teaspoonful.

Use shiny cookie sheets at least two inches smaller than the oven. This allows heat to circulate and the cookies to brown evenly.

Don't use hot cookie sheets, just out of the oven, or cookies will spread.

For most even browning, bake one pan of cookies at a time with the rack in the center of the oven.

If you think your oven temperature isn't accurate (and many ovens are not), experiment by baking two or three cookies at various temperatures to see what works best.

Remove cookies with a thin edged pancake turner as soon as they come out of the oven or as the recipe directs. This prevents overbaking.

Learn from the judges' comments and try again, if you don't win the first time.

Storing Cookies

Cool cookies completely before storing or they will soften. Store soft and chewy cookies in containers with tight-fitting lids.

Keep crisp cookies in containers with loose-fitting lids. If cookies are fragile, place waxed paper between layers. If crisp cookies become soft, heat them in a 300F (150C) oven for 5 minutes to recrisp.

Don't mix soft and crisp cookies in the same container. The crisp ones will soften.

If bar cookies will be eaten in a day or two, store them in the baking pan covered with foil.

Cookies freeze well. Use containers with tight lids or tightly sealed plastic bags. Crisp cookies break easily when they are frozen. Cushion the layers with waxed paper. Thaw cookies in their container at room temperature.

A few cookies or bars also can be thawed in the microwave on a paper plate or napkin. The time will depend upon the sugar and fat content of the cookies.

Chocolate Guidelines

If the recipe calls for melting chocolate with additional fat, you can melt it over very low heat. Stir frequently and remove it from the heat before the chocolate is completely melted. Then stir until it is smooth.

When melting chocolate by itself, use the top of a double boiler over simmering (not boiling) water. If the amount needed is too small to make a double boiler practical, use a small bowl inside a saucepan containing about 1/2 inch of hot water. *Do not let any moisture get into the chocolate or it will all harden.*

Melting chocolate in a microwave works well. Use 100% (HIGH) power for chips and for squares melted with additional fat. Use 50% (MEDIUM) power for squares melted alone. Melt the chocolate in a measuring cup or microwave bowl and stir at least once to prevent scorching. Do not cover.

Chips and squares of semisweet chocolate can be substituted for each other when the recipe calls for melted chocolate. Use six ounces of semisweet chocolate chips for six (one-ounce) squares.

Different brands of chocolate squares and chips can vary in the way they melt. When you find a brand that works well for you, stick with it when results are important.

Oatmeal Brickle Cookies

Rose Datko waited until she was 85 years old to enter the Minnesota State Fair. Then she made up for lost time by winning three ribbons, including a blue ribbon for her cookies. The addition of golden raisins, almond brickle baking chips and a generous amount of chopped walnuts gives these rich, sweet cookies a distinctive flavor and takes them out of the kids' snack category.

1 cup butter, room temperature
1 cup granulated sugar
1 cup firmly packed brown sugar
2 eggs, beaten
1 teaspoon vanilla extract
1-1/2 cups all-purpose flour
1/2 teaspoon salt
1 teaspoon baking soda
3 cups regular rolled oats
2 cups golden raisins
1-1/4 cups chopped walnuts
1 (6-oz.) package almond brickle baking chips

Preheat oven to 350F (175C). Lightly grease several baking sheets. In a large bowl, cream butter and sugars until light and fluffy. Beat in eggs and vanilla. In a medium-size bowl, combine flour, salt and baking soda; blend into creamed mixture. Stir in oats, raisins, walnuts and baking chips, mixing well. Drop by level tablespoonfuls 2 inches apart onto greased baking sheets. Bake in preheated oven 13 to 15 minutes or just until golden brown. Do not overbake. Cool cookies on baking sheets 1 minute, then remove from baking sheets to wire racks to cool. Makes 78 cookies.

Rose M. Datko   St. Paul, Minnesota   Minnesota State Fair

Sweet Chocolate Drop Cookies

Once Denise Turnbull had won best bread of show and grand championship for bread in the Illinois State Fair culinary arts contests, she decided it was time to try out her cookie skills. Starting with a whole-wheat chocolate chip cookie recipe, she experimented until she had developed a rich, chewy drop cookie with a mild, sweet chocolate flavor. Large granules of pearl sugar make an attractive baked-on topping.

1 (6-oz.) package semisweet chocolate chips
1 cup butter or margarine, room temperature
2/3 cup granulated sugar
2/3 cup firmly packed brown sugar
1 egg, beaten
2 teaspoons vanilla extract
2-1/4 cups all-purpose flour
1/2 teaspoon salt
1 teaspoon baking powder
Pearl sugar, if desired

Preheat oven to 375F (190C). Melt chocolate chips in top of double boiler set over a pan of simmering water; cool. In a large bowl, cream butter and sugars until creamy. Beat in egg and vanilla. Stir in melted chocolate until well blended. Sift flour, salt and baking powder into a medium-size bowl. Stir dry ingredients into chocolate mixture until thoroughly combined. Drop by level tablespoonfuls 2 inches apart on ungreased baking sheets. Pat in round shapes. Sprinkle with pearl sugar, if desired. Bake in preheated oven about 12 minutes or until cookies are set. Makes 48 cookies.

Denise M. Turnbull   Monmouth, Illinois   Illinois State Fair

Chocolate Nut Refrigerator Cookies

For a busy professional like Mary Schuman, who is a district director in the Indiana Cooperative Extension Service, refrigerator cookies are ideal because they can be made in short blocks of time. She can mix the dough in a few minutes after work, refrigerate it and bake the cookies when she needs them in the next day or two.

1-1/2 cups sifted all-purpose flour
1/2 cup unsweetened cocoa powder
1/2 teaspoon baking soda
1/2 teaspoon salt
2/3 cup margarine
1 cup sugar
1 egg
1 teaspoon vanilla extract
2 tablespoons milk
1 cup chopped walnuts

Sift flour, cocoa powder, baking soda and salt into a medium-size bowl. In a large bowl, cream margarine and sugar until light and fluffy. Add egg and vanilla; beat well. Add dry ingredients alternately with milk to creamed mixture, mixing well after each addition. Stir in walnuts. Cover and chill dough in refrigerator at least 2 hours. Divide dough in half. Shape each half in a 7-inch roll about 1-1/2 inches in diameter. Wrap rolls tightly in waxed paper or plastic wrap. Chill in refrigerator overnight. Preheat oven to 375F (190C). Lightly grease several baking sheets. Using a sharp knife, cut rolls in 1/4-inch slices, dipping knife in cold water occasionally for a cleaner cut. If kitchen is warm, refrigerate second roll while cutting first. Place slices about 1-1/2 inches apart on greased baking sheets. Bake in preheated oven 8 minutes or until tops are just set. Remove cookies from baking sheets to wire racks to cool. Makes about 48 cookies.

Mary E. Shuman   Indianapolis, Indiana   Indiana State Fair

Snappy Molasses Crinkles

An artist with food, Lena Forbis decorates cakes and does catering in addition to working full-time and raising three children. Everyone who loves old-fashioned crinkle-topped gingersnaps will rejoice in her recipe. These are like a superior version of commercial gingersnaps, with a crisp but chewy texture and a marvelous spicy flavor.

2-1/4 cups all-purpose flour
1 teaspoon baking soda
1 teaspoon ground cinnamon
1 teaspoon ground ginger
1/2 teaspoon ground cloves
1/8 teaspoon salt
1 cup firmly packed brown sugar
3/4 cup shortening
1/4 cup molasses
1 egg
Granulated sugar

Preheat oven to 375F (190C). Sift flour, soda, spices and salt into a medium-size bowl. In a large bowl, beat brown sugar, shortening, molasses and egg until well blended. Stir dry ingredients into creamed mixture until well blended. Cover and refrigerate at least 1 hour. Shape dough in balls about 1 inch in diameter. Roll in granulated sugar. Place on ungreased baking sheets 3 inches apart. Bake in preheated oven 10 to 12 minutes or until set and tops have cracked. Makes about 48 cookies.

Lena Forbis   Louisville, Kentucky   Kentucky State Fair

High-Fiber Oatmeal Cookies

Wonderful flavor plus nutritious ingredients make Kristyn Drew's oatmeal cookies a family favorite for snacks or a simple dessert with fruit. Unprocessed bran, available in health food stores and co-ops, add extra fiber and an elusive, delicious "wheaty" flavor to the cookies. The Drews moved from Des Moines to Omaha soon after she won her Iowa State Fair blue ribbon.

1 cup butter, room temperature
1/2 cup granulated sugar
1 cup firmly packed brown sugar
1 egg
1 teaspoon vanilla extract
2 cups quick-cooking rolled oats
1 cup unprocessed (miller's) bran
1 cup all-purpose flour
1 teaspoon salt
1/2 teaspoon baking soda
1 cup raisins
2/3 cup shredded carrot
    (about 1 medium-size)

Preheat oven to 350F (175C). In a large bowl, cream butter and sugars until fluffy. Beat in egg and vanilla. Add oats, bran, flour, salt and baking soda; mix until well blended. Stir in raisins and shredded carrot. Drop dough by teaspoonfuls on ungreased baking sheets. Bake in preheated oven about 12 minutes or until firm and lightly browned. Makes about 108 small cookies or 72 medium-size cookies.

Kristyn L. Drews   Omaha, Nebraska   Iowa State Fair

Oatmeal-Raisin Crinkles

Spurred on by his wife's success at the Ohio State Fair, Charles Hildreth decided to bake a batch of favorite oatmeal cookies and enter them. Result: two Hildreth first prize winners. A pleasant change from the usual oatmeal drop cookie, this is a flat, butter-flavored cookie with the good chewy texture typical of a crinkle type of cookie. They spread while baking, so for shapely rounds, place the balls of dough at least two inches apart.

1/2 cup butter, room temperature
1/2 cup margarine, room temperature
2-1/3 cups sugar
2 eggs
1 teaspoon vanilla extract
1 cup regular rolled oats
1 cup chopped raisins
2-3/4 cups sifted all-purpose flour
1-1/2 teaspoons soda
1/4 teaspoon salt

Preheat oven to 350F (175C). In a large bowl, cream butter, margarine and 2 cups of sugar until fluffy. Beat in eggs and vanilla. In a medium-size bowl, combine oats, raisins, flour, soda and salt. Stir oat mixture into creamed mixture. Shape level tablespoonfuls of dough in balls; roll in remaining 1/3 cup of sugar. Arrange 2 inches apart on ungreased baking sheets. Bake in preheated oven 10 to 12 minutes or until golden brown. Makes 48 cookies.

Charles Hildreth   Fairborn, Ohio   Ohio State Fair

Simple Sesame Slices

Donna Plowman is known as "The Cookiebaker," and these enticing cookies are a good example of how she earned her title. After 27 years in Alaska, she and her husband Duncan have retired in Missouri where she keeps her freezer stocked with cookies for her grandchildren. Long baking in a slow oven makes these buttery sliced refrigerator cookies extra crunchy and develops the toasted sesame seed flavor. For neat slices it is important to chop the almonds fine. A knife can't cut through a big chunk.

2 cups butter, room temperature
1-1/2 cups sugar
3 cups all-purpose flour
1 cup sesame seeds
2 cups shredded coconut
1/2 cup finely chopped almonds
1/2 cup sliced almonds

In a large bowl, cream butter. Gradually add sugar and continue beating until light and fluffy. Add flour and mix just until combined. Stir in sesame seeds, coconut and chopped almonds just until well mixed. Divide dough in thirds. Place 1 piece of dough on a long sheet of waxed paper. Shape in a long roll 2 inches in diameter. Press 1/3 of sliced almonds on top of roll. Repeat with remaining dough. Wrap and refrigerate until firm. Preheat oven to 300F (150C). Cut each roll in 24 (1/4-inch) slices; place on ungreased baking sheets. Bake in preheated oven 25 to 30 minutes or until edges are golden brown and cookies are set. Cool 1 minute. Carefully remove cookies to wire racks to cool. Makes about 72 cookies.

Donna Plowman   Mountain Grove, Missouri   Ozark Empire Fair

Peanut Butter Cookies

When 24 expert cooks using similar recipes compete for the best peanut butter cookies, other cookie bakers value tips from the winner. Georgia Crawford, who has collected many ribbons for cookies at the Illinois fair, always uses chunky peanut butter and light-brown sugar. She also warns against overbaking, as these rich cookies scorch easily. Her cookies are crunchy, rather than crisp, and have a rich peanut-butter flavor with the bonus of bits of chopped peanuts. The soft dough needs to be refrigerated before forming the cookies. Because they spread while baking, place them three inches apart on the baking sheet for perfectly-shaped round cookies.

1/2 cup margarine
1/2 cup chunky-style peanut butter
1/2 cup granulated sugar
1/2 cup firmly packed light-brown sugar
1 egg
1/2 teaspoon vanilla extract
1-1/4 cups all-purpose flour
1/2 teaspoon baking powder
3/4 teaspoon baking soda
1/4 teaspoon salt
All-purpose flour or granulated sugar

Preheat oven to 375F (190C). Lightly grease several baking sheets. In a large bowl, combine margarine, peanut butter, 1/2 cup granulated sugar, brown sugar, egg and vanilla thoroughly. In a medium-size bowl, mix flour, baking powder, baking soda and salt. Add to peanut butter mixture, mixing thoroughly. Chill dough about 3 hours. Roll level tablespoonfuls of dough in 1-1/4-inch balls. Place 3 inches apart on greased baking sheet. Using a fork dipped into flour or sugar, flatten dough crisscross style. Bake in preheated oven 10 to 12 minutes or until slightly brown. Makes 36 cookies.

Georgia L. Crawford Jacksonville, Illinois   Illinois State Fair

High-Fiber Oatmeal Drop Cookies

Ursula Maurer overcame having no sense of smell and a limited ability to taste food by her intelligent approach to cooking. Besides using the highest quality ingredients and relying on her family's critical judgment as tasters, the former high school teacher applies her knowledge of food chemistry when she adapts recipes. When she started entering the fair competitions, she watched the judging and learned what counted most in the judging criteria. She wrote down baking tips from the judges and observed what kind of recipes won. For her nutritious drop cookie, entered in a high-fiber, low-sugar class, she used her skills to develop a winning combination of great flavor and texture. Loaded with fruit and nuts, the cookies taste even better the second day and keep well.

1/2 cup raisins
1 cup water
1-1/2 cups whole-wheat flour
1/2 teaspoon baking soda
1/2 teaspoon salt
1 teaspoon ground cinnamon
1 tablespoon cultured buttermilk powder
1 tablespoon unprocessed (miller's) bran
1-3/4 cups regular rolled oats
1/2 cup finely chopped prunes or dried apricots
1/2 cup unsalted roasted sunflower nuts
1/2 cup chopped walnuts
1 egg
1/3 cup safflower or corn oil
1/2 cup honey

🎖 Preheat oven to 350F (175C). Grease several baking sheets. In a small saucepan, simmer raisins and water 5 minutes. Drain, reserving 1/4 cup of liquid. In a large bowl, combine flour, baking soda, salt, cinnamon, buttermilk powder and bran thoroughly. Add oats, drained raisins, prunes and nuts. In a small bowl, beat reserved raisin liquid, egg, oil and honey until well blended. Add to oat mixture and mix well. Drop by level tablespoonfuls onto greased baking sheets. Bake in preheated oven 12 to 15 minutes or until cookies are slightly brown on edges and tops are set. Do not overbake. Remove cookies from baking sheets to wire racks to cool. Makes about 42 cookies.

Ursula Maurer   Wauwatosa, Wisconsin   Wisconsin State Fair

Mrs. S's Date-Filled Oatmeal Cookies

For midwesterners, these date-filled cookies will bring back memories of cookies and milk in the kitchen after school or visits to grandma on baking day. Bonnie Lillemon got her recipe for these wonderful homey cookies from her sister, then went on to win a blue ribbon with it. Although less experienced cookie bakers shy away from making rolled cookies, the oatmeal dough is not difficult to handle. The unusual half-moon shape is formed by folding the round cookie in half over the date filling.

1 (1-lb.) package pitted dates, finely cut
1 cup granulated sugar
1 cup water
3/4 cup chopped walnuts
1 cup margarine
1-1/2 cups firmly packed brown sugar
2 eggs
1 teaspoon vanilla extract
1-1/2 cups regular rolled oats
3-1/4 cups all-purpose flour
1 teaspoon baking soda
1 teaspoon cream of tartar
1/2 teaspoon salt

In a medium-size saucepan, combine dates, granulated sugar and water. Bring to a boil over medium heat. Boil 2 minutes, stirring constantly. Remove from heat and beat with a spoon until well blended. Stir in walnuts; cool. In a large bowl, cream margarine and brown sugar until well blended. Beat in eggs and vanilla until mixture is light and fluffy. Stir in oats. In a medium-size bowl, combine flour, baking soda, cream of tartar and salt. Stir dry ingredients into creamed mixture; mix until well blended. Chill dough about 1 hour for easier handling. Preheat oven to 375F (190C). Remove 1/4 of dough at a time; refrigerate remainder of dough. On a lightly floured board or pastry cloth, roll dough 1/8-inch thick. Cut rounds with a 2-1/2-inch cookie cutter. Place rounds 1 inch apart on ungreased baking sheets. Spoon 1 teaspoon of date mixture near center of each cookie. Using back of a table knife, lift 1 side of cookie and fold it over other half. Edges will seal as cookies bake. Bake in preheated oven 8 to 10 minutes or until cookies are light golden brown. Remove cookies from baking sheet and cool on wire racks. Repeat with remaining dough and filling. Makes 48 cookies.

Bonnie Lillemon   Minot, North Dakota   North Dakota State Fair

Lemon-Filled Sandwich Cookies

When she was a television meteorologist in Louisville, Kentucky, Laura York won ribbons and the sweepstakes award for cookies at the Kentucky State Fair. After the fair she was able to share her prize winning recipes with her viewers. A few years later, she and her husband moved to Florida in time to enter that fair, which is held in Tampa in February. Lemon-Filled Sandwich Cookies, her "all time favorite" cookie, brought another sweepstakes rosette.

2 eggs
1/2 cup sugar
1/2 cup butter, softened
1 tablespoon water
1 teaspoon vanilla extract
1-1/2 cups all-purpose flour
1/2 teaspoon salt
1/4 teaspoon baking soda
3/4 cup chopped pecans

Lemon Filling:

1 cup powdered sugar
2 teaspoons butter, softened
1 teaspoon grated lemon peel
4-1/2 teaspoons lemon juice

Separate eggs, dropping yolks into a large bowl and whites into a small bowl. Refrigerate whites. Add sugar, butter, water and vanilla to yolks; mix thoroughly. Stir in flour, salt and baking soda. Divide dough in half. Shape each piece in a 7" x 1-1/2" roll. Wrap in foil or plastic wrap. Refrigerate about 4 hours or until firm. Preheat oven to 400F (205C). Cut each roll in 1/8-inch slices. Place slices 1-inch apart on ungreased baking sheets. Beat chilled egg whites slightly with a fork;

stir in pecans. Spoon 1/2 teaspoon of pecan mixture in a mound on 1/2 of cookie slices. Bake in preheated oven about 6 minutes or until edges begin to brown. Remove cookies immediately to a wire rack to cool. Prepare Lemon Filling. Spread filling on plain cookies. Use pecan-topped cookies for tops. Makes about 48 sandwich cookies.

Lemon Filling:

In a small bowl, mix powdered sugar, butter and lemon peel and juice until smooth.

Laura Case York   Valrico, Florida   Florida State Fair

Coconut Macaroons

Law student Bill Kuntz moved into state fair exhibiting after years as a 4-H Club member and leader. As a member he won state and national baking demonstration awards. More recently he has judged 4-H contests at the state fair and at many county fairs. His light, airy meringue cookies will keep for at least two weeks in a tightly-sealed container.

2 egg whites
1/8 teaspoon salt
1/2 teaspoon vanilla extract
2/3 cup sugar
2 cups flaked coconut

Preheat oven to 350F (175C). Grease 2 baking sheets. In a large bowl, beat egg whites and salt at high speed just until soft peaks begin to form. Add vanilla and very gradually add sugar, beating constantly until stiff peaks form. Fold in coconut. Drop meringue by tablespoonfuls 2 inches apart onto greased baking sheets. Bake in preheated oven about 20 minutes or until lightly browned. Cool 1 minute, then carefully remove from baking sheets. Makes 20 cookies.

Bill Kuntz   Indianapolis, Indiana   Indiana State Fair

Nitey-Nite Cookies

"So easy my 9-year-old daughter enjoys making them" is Lynne Boyers' comment about her melt-in-the-mouth cookies, which are sometimes called forgotten meringues. They bake overnight in the oven which has been preheated, turned off and left closed until morning. Since the cookies are quick to make, turn the oven on 10 to 15 minutes before you expect to bake them.

    2 egg whites, room temperature
    2/3 cup sugar
    1 cup chopped pecans
    1 (6-oz.) package semisweet chocolate pieces

Preheat oven to 350F (175C). Line a baking sheet with parchment paper or foil. In a medium-size bowl, beat egg whites until frothy. Gradually add sugar a little at a time, beating until mixture holds stiff peaks. Fold in pecans and chocolate pieces. Drop by teaspoonfuls 2 inches apart on prepared baking sheet. Place in preheated oven, quickly close door and turn off oven. Let cookies remain overnight or at least 5 hours. Do not open oven door until cookies are baked. Makes 30 cookies.

Lynne Boyers   Tampa, Florida   Florida State Fair

Pecan Tassies

Like many state fair exhibitors across the country, Virginia Lawson says, "Once my name was called at judging and I received a blue ribbon, I was hooked." Her prize-winning Pecan Tassies are like four-bite pecan pies. The easily-made cream cheese crust is pressed into tiny tart pans, then filled with the pecan mixture and baked. Mrs. Lawson likes to serve them for tea. If you don't have as many as 24 miniature muffin cups or tiny tart pans, bake one batch, remove the cookies, chill the pans briefly in the freezer and repeat.

1 (3-oz.) package cream cheese, room temperature
1/2 cup butter or margarine, room temperature
1 cup sifted all-purpose flour
1 cup chopped pecans
1 egg
3/4 cup firmly packed brown sugar
1 tablespoon butter
1 teaspoon vanilla extract

In a medium-size bowl, combine cream cheese and butter. Stir in flour and blend well. Cover bowl and chill dough about 1 hour. Preheat oven to 325F (165C). Shape dough in 1-inch balls. Place balls in 24 (1-3/4-inch) ungreased muffin tins or in tiny tart pans. Press dough evenly over bottom and sides of cups. Arrange chopped pecans in each tart shell, using about 1/2 cup. In a small bowl, beat egg, brown sugar, butter and vanilla just until blended. Spoon filling into shells; sprinkle remaining 1/2 cup chopped pecans over filling. Bake in preheated oven 25 minutes or until light golden brown and filling is set. Let stand 5 minutes, then remove from pans. Makes 24 cookie tarts.

Virginia Lawson   Albuquerque, New Mexico   New Mexico State Fair

Fig-Raisin Crescents

Cookies are a passion of Fran Neavoll, who collects cookie cookbooks and cutters. She tries out new recipes all during the year to find the perfect recipe to enter in the state fair. Fig-Raisin Crescents is her adaptation of an Italian pastry. Ground dried fruit and almonds are the filling for a pliable cookie dough which is formed into crescents. The baked pastries are frosted and garnished with almonds.

2-1/2 cups all-purpose flour
1/3 cup sugar
1/4 teaspoon baking powder
10 tablespoons butter
1/2 cup milk
1 egg, beaten
3/4 cup golden raisins
1 (8-oz.) package dried figs (1-1/2 cups)
3/4 cup slivered almonds
1/4 cup sugar
1/4 cup hot water
1/4 teaspoon ground cinnamon

Almond Butter Frosting:

1 cup powdered sugar, sifted
2 tablespoons butter, softened
1/4 teaspoon almond extract
1 to 2 tablespoons cream

In a medium-size bowl, combine flour, 1/3 cup sugar and baking powder. Using a pastry blender or fingertips, cut in butter until mixture is crumbly. Stir in milk and egg until well mixed. Divide dough in fourths, wrap in plastic wrap and chill thoroughly, about 2 hours. Preheat oven to 350F (175C). In a food processor or grinder, grind raisins, figs and 1/4 cup of almonds. In a small bowl, combine ground fruits and nuts, 1/4 cup sugar, water and cinnamon. Between 2 pieces waxed paper, roll out 1 piece of chilled dough 1/8 inch thick using a rolling pin. Cut in 3" x 2" rectangles. Place 1 tablespoonful of filling along short side of rectangle. Roll up starting with short side. Place seam side down on ungreased baking sheet. Curve in ends to form a crescent. Using a sharp knife, make 3 small cuts in outer curve of crescent. Repeat with remaining dough and filling. Bake in pre-heated oven about 20 minutes or until golden brown; cool. Prepare Almond Butter Frosting. Spread tops and sides of cookies with frosting. Garnish tops of cookies with remaining 1/2 cup of almonds. Makes 48 cookies.

Almond Butter Frosting:

In a small bowl, mix powdered sugar, butter, almond extract and enough cream to make a smooth spreadable frosting.

Fran Neavoll   Salem, Oregon   Oregon State Fair

Festive Honey-Fruit Bars

Keeping bees is a hobby or entrepreneurial venture for farmers and suburbanites alike. Almost every state recognizes this with honey judging contests and entries for baking which use honey as the only sweetener. Many good honey recipes have been developed for fair competition, like these quickly-made fruit bars. Suzanne Skeeters is an enthusiastic exhibitor who always has some baked treat ready at home for her husband and three children. Like most baking made with honey, these rich, moist bars develop even more flavor after a day or two. They keep well in a tightly-covered container.

1/4 cup margarine, softened
1/3 cup honey
2 eggs, beaten
2/3 cup sifted all-purpose flour
1/2 teaspoon baking powder
1/2 teaspoon salt
1/2 cup chopped walnuts
1/4 cup raisins
1 cup chopped dates
1/2 cup chopped candied cherries or well-drained
* maraschino cherries*
Powdered sugar

Preheat oven to 300F (150C). Grease and flour an 8-inch-square baking pan. In a medium-size bowl, beat margarine and honey until well mixed; beat in eggs. In a small bowl, mix flour, baking powder and salt; add to creamed mixture, mixing until well blended. Stir in nuts and fruit. Pour into prepared pan. Bake in preheated oven 35 to 45 minutes or until a wooden pick inserted into center comes out clean. Cool in pan on a wire rack. Cut in 20 bars. Sprinkle lightly with powdered sugar and remove from pan. Store tightly covered. Bars will mellow and develop flavor after 1 day. Makes 20 bars.

Suzanne R. Skeeters Springfield, Illinois Illinois State Fair

Lemon Bars

When Donna Morgan arrives with other contestants to leave food and greet the staff of the home arts department at the New Mexico State Fair each year, she says it's like old home week. After 11 years of exhibiting, she still considers the fair the highlight of her year. Lemon Bars is one of many entries which have brought her blue ribbons. The tangy layered bars are elegant enough to serve at receptions or teas. Best when freshly- made, leftovers can be frozen.

1 cup butter, softened
Dash salt
1/2 cup powdered sugar
2-1/4 cups sifted all-purpose flour
2 cups granulated sugar
4 eggs, beaten
6 tablespoons lemon juice
Powdered sugar

Preheat oven to 350F (175C). In a medium-size bowl, combine butter, salt, 1/2 cup powdered sugar and 2 cups of flour; mix well. Press firmly into a 13" x 9" ungreased baking pan. Bake in preheated oven 15 to 20 minutes or until light golden brown; cool. In a medium-size bowl, combine remaining 1/4 cup of flour and granulated sugar. Stir in eggs and lemon juice. Pour onto partially-baked crust. Bake 25 minutes or until a wooden pick inserted into center comes out clean. Edges will brown before center is set. Cool; sift powdered sugar over top. Cut in bars. Makes 36 bars.

Donna M. Morgan   Albuquerque, N. Mexico   N. Mexico State Fair

Dream Bars

Anna Marie Davis owns 500 cookbooks and has a four-drawer file full of recipes. But when she wants one of her family's favorites, she turns to their personal computer where they are stored. Many of these are winning recipes from the fair, as well as other recipe and baking contests she has entered. Her Dream Bars were judged best of class, in addition to winning a blue ribbon. While there are a number of variations of these popular two-layer bars, basically they all combine a buttery cookie crust with a rich coconut-walnut batter.

1/2 cup butter
1/2 cup firmly packed brown sugar
1 cup all-purpose flour
1-1/2 cups shredded coconut
1 cup chopped walnuts
2 tablespoons all-purpose flour
1/4 teaspoon salt
1 teaspoon baking powder
2 eggs
1 cup firmly packed brown sugar
2 teaspoons vanilla extract
Powdered sugar

Preheat oven to 375F (190C). In a medium-size bowl, mix butter, 1/2 cup brown sugar and 1 cup flour with fingertips or fork until crumbly. Pat into a 12" x 8" baking pan, covering bottom evenly. Bake in preheated oven 10 minutes; cool. Meanwhile, in a food processor or blender, chop coconut in 1/2-inch pieces. In a small bowl, mix coconut, walnuts, 2 tablespoons flour, salt and baking powder. In a medium-size bowl, beat eggs, 1 cup brown sugar and vanilla. Fold coconut mixture into creamed mixture. Pour over cooled crust, spreading evenly. Bake 20 minutes or until golden brown and filling is set. Cool slightly. While still warm, using a sharp knife, cut in 48 (2" x 3/4") bars. Cool in pan. Sift powdered sugar over bars. Makes 48 bars.

Anna Marie Davis   Fair Oaks, California   California State Fair

Nut & Raisin Dream Bars

Sandra Herzog is a recent state fair exhibitor, but an expert baker, who has won blue ribbons both years. Entering the first time for the learning experience of having her baking judged by experts, she quickly realized that a rich, moist baked product has a better chance of winning, because food sometimes stands uncovered for hours before judging. Her luscious, two-layer bars fit that description, with the bonus of being quick and easy to make.

1 cup all-purpose flour
1/2 cup firmly packed brown sugar
1/2 cup butter
1/4 cup all-purpose flour
1/2 cup firmly packed brown sugar
2 eggs, slightly beaten
1/2 cup dark corn syrup
1 teaspoon vanilla extract
1/4 teaspoon salt
1 cup chopped pecans
1/2 cup flaked coconut
1/2 cup raisins

Preheat oven to 350F (175C). In a small bowl, combine 1 cup flour and 1/2 cup brown sugar. Using a pastry blender or 2 knives, cut in butter to make fine crumbs. Pat into an ungreased 8-inch-square baking pan. Bake in preheated oven 20 minutes. Meanwhile, in a medium-size bowl, combine 1/4 cup flour and 1/2 cup brown sugar. Beat in eggs, corn syrup, vanilla and salt until mixture is smooth. Fold in pecans, coconut and raisins. Carefully spread over hot partially-baked crust. Bake 30 minutes more or until top is golden brown and filling has set. Cool in pan on a wire rack. When lukewarm, cut with a sharp knife into bars. Makes 16 to 24 bars.

Sandra Herzog   Wauwatosa, Wisconsin   Wisconsin State Fair

Mocha Walnut Bars

Beth Taticek first brought baking to the Wisconsin fair when she was 16. She won a blue ribbon and every year since has looked forward to finding new recipes to enter. Now her husband's co-workers also eagerly anticipate fair time, because they get to taste test the recipes she considers entering. They and the fair judges all decided these rich bars were a winner.

1-1/2 cups sifted all-purpose flour
1 teaspoon baking powder
1/4 teaspoon baking soda
1/4 teaspoon salt
1/2 teaspoon ground cinnamon
1/4 cup butter, room temperature
1 cup firmly packed brown sugar
1 egg
1/2 cup strong coffee
1/2 cup raisins
1-1/2 cups chopped walnuts
1/2 cup semisweet chocolate pieces
3 ounces white confectioner's coating, if desired

Preheat oven to 350F (175C). Generously grease a 13" x 9" baking pan. Sift flour, baking powder, baking soda, salt and cinnamon into a small bowl. In a large bowl, cream butter, brown sugar and egg until very light and fluffy. Add dry ingredients alternately with coffee, stirring to mix well. Stir in raisins and 1 cup of chopped walnuts. Spread batter in greased pan. Sprinkle with remaining 1/2 cup of walnuts and chocolate pieces. Bake in preheated oven 20 to 25 minutes or until top springs back when lightly touched. Cool to barely warm in pan on a wire rack. Cut in 30 diamond shapes. If desired, melt confectioner's coating in top of a double boiler set over hot, not boiling, water. Spoon into a pastry bag fitted with a small round tip. Pipe designs over each bar. Carefully remove bars from pan. Makes 30 bars.

Beth Taticek   Delafield, Wisconsin   Wisconsin State Fair

Crunchy Pecan Bars

When Marilyn Martell started exhibiting at her local county fair, she won so many ribbons for cookies that she decided to share them in a cookbook entitled "County Fair Prize Cookies", published in 1975. For a number of years now, she has competed at the state fair, continuing to win blue ribbons for baking. Crunchy Pecan Bars is a long-time favorite. The delectable toffee-flavored bars are quick to make and yield a large batch. Simply pat the dough into a jelly-roll pan. Long baking at a low temperature gives the thin bars their crisp texture. They keep well—if you hide them.

1 cup butter, room temperature
1 cup sugar
1 egg, separated
1 teaspoon vanilla extract
2 cups all-purpose flour
1 teaspoon ground cinnamon
1-1/2 cups sliced pecans
Sugar

Preheat oven to 275F (135C). Butter a 15" x 10" jelly-roll pan. In a large bowl, cream butter and sugar until light and fluffy. Add egg yolk and vanilla; mix well. In a medium-size bowl, mix flour and cinnamon. Stir flour mixture into creamed mixture, using hands to mix stiff dough, if necessary. Spread evenly in buttered jelly-roll pan. In a small bowl, beat egg white just until well mixed; spread over dough. Sprinkle pecans evenly over top, then sprinkle lightly with sugar. Bake in preheated oven about 1 hour or until set. Cut in 2" x 1" bars or diamond shapes while still very warm. Remove cookies from baking sheet to wire racks and cool. Cookies become crisp as they cool. Makes about 72 cookies.

Marilyn Martell   Reedley, California   *California State Fair*

Filled Chocolate Madeleines

Suzanne Kopf is an artist with food who has decorated cakes and made ginger-bread houses for magazine photographs, television shows and commercial displays. She also is a talented cook who has won many ribbons for baking and candy. Her Filled Chocolate Madeleines combine both skills. She puts together two of the little shell-shaped cakes with a rich butter cream filling in such a way that it looks like a partially-opened sea shell. Recipe directions explain how to achieve this effect. Her recipe calls for the small (1-1/2-inch) Madeleine molds. If you own the larger traditional-size pans, your finished product will be cake-size, rather than cookie-size. The tender, deep chocolate Madeleine cookies also are scrumptious without embellishment. She prefers unsalted butter for baking, but any high quality butter will give good results in the recipe.

10 tablespoons unsalted sweet butter
3 ounces semisweet chocolate
2 tablespoons unsweetened cocoa powder
3/4 cup sugar
1-1/4 cup sifted all-purpose flour
1/8 teaspoon salt
3 eggs, room temperature
2 egg yolks
1 teaspoon vanilla extract
2 ounces semisweet chocolate, melted

Butter Cream Filling:

1/2 cup unsalted sweet butter, room temperature
1 (1-lb.) box powdered sugar
1 teaspoon vanilla extract
About 2 teaspoons milk

🎀 Preheat oven to 350F (175C). Spray small (1-1/2 inch) Madeleine molds with cooking spray or generously grease and flour. If using only 1 pan, cooking spray will save the time of washing and regreasing molds between each baking. In a small saucepan, melt butter and chocolate over low heat, stirring to blend. Sift cocoa powder, sugar, flour and salt into a medium-size bowl. In a small bowl, beat or whisk eggs, egg yolks and vanilla until eggs are light and fluffy. Blend melted chocolate mixture and eggs into flour mixture. Stir about 2 minutes or until sugar is thoroughly incorporated. Fill greased molds *1/2 full*. Cakes should have a flat surface on top, not a rounded top. Bake in preheated oven about 5 minutes or until a wooden pick inserted into a cake comes out clean. Remove cake from pan to a wire rack, shell side up, to cool. Repeat with remaining batter, spraying pan with cooking spray between batches. As cakes cool, immediately place in an airtight container or plastic bags to prevent from drying out. Prepare Butter Cream Filling. Spread about 1-1/2 teaspoons of filling between each pair of cakes, with shell side out, putting a little more filling at top to give effect of a slightly opened sea shell. Refrigerate in covered containers to firm filling. Brush melted chocolate on top side of each filled cookie. Refrigerate in covered containers or freeze. To serve, let stand about 15 minutes at room temperature. Makes about 84 Madeleines or 42 filled cookies.

Butter Cream Filling:

In a medium-size bowl, cream butter, powdered sugar and vanilla until very well blended. Add enough milk to make a spreadable filling.

VARIATION If using traditional-size pans, bake Madeleines about 10 minutes or until a wooden pick inserted into a cake comes out clean. To make unfilled Chocolate Madeleines, fill molds about 2/3 full. Makes about 42 Madeleines or 21 filled cookies.

Suzanne Kopf   Westerville, Ohio   Ohio State Fair

Chocolate Crackles

As attractive as they are good tasting, Chocolate Crackles were one of the five different cookies included in Margo Shull's prestigious Orark Empire Cookie Jar award. Balls of chilled chocolate cookie dough are heavily coated with powdered sugar. The sugar bakes on, forming a macaroon-like contrast to the crackle-topped dark chocolate cookie. These rich cookies quickly over-bake, becoming hard rather than chewy, so time the baking carefully for best results.

2 cups semisweet chocolate pieces, melted
2 cups firmly packed brown sugar
2/3 cup vegetable oil
4 eggs
2 teaspoons vanilla extract
2 cups all-purpose flour
2 teaspoons baking powder
1/2 teaspoon salt
1 cup chopped walnuts
2/3 cup sifted powdered sugar

Preheat oven to 350F (175C). Lightly grease several baking sheets. In a large bowl, combine melted chocolate, brown sugar and oil, beating until well blended. Add eggs, 1 at a time, beating after each addition. Stir in vanilla. In a medium-size bowl, mix flour, baking powder and salt. Blend into chocolate mixture. Add walnuts, stirring just enough to blend ingredients. Cover bowl and refrigerate dough at least 2 hours. Roll level tablespoonfuls of dough in balls. Drop into powdered sugar and roll to coat heavily. Place 2 inches apart on greased baking sheets. Dough is soft; if kitchen is warm, divide dough in half and refrigerate 1 half while forming 1/2 of balls. Bake in preheated oven 10 to 12 minutes or until tops are slightly puffed, crackled and just set. Makes 72 cookies.

Margo J. Shull   Springfield, Missouri   Ozark Empire Fair

Pignolia-Topped Almond Wafers

The flavor of these elegant little cookies will remind you of the Italian almond-flavored macaroons, amaretti. The crunchy wafers are nice to serve with ice cream or fruit. Paula Pezzi likes to top them with pignolia (pine nuts). If these little imported nuts are not available, substitute almonds.

1 (8-oz.) can almond paste
2 egg whites
1/2 cup granulated sugar
1/2 cup powdered sugar
1/4 cup all-purpose flour
Dash salt
Additional granulated sugar
3 ounces pignolia (pine nuts) or 1/3 cup sliced blanched almonds

Preheat oven to 300F (150C). Generously grease several baking sheets. In a medium-size bowl, break almond paste in pieces with a fork. Add egg whites and beat until very well blended. Sift sugars, flour and salt into almond paste mixture. Blend thoroughly. Chill dough about 1 hour. Roll rounded teaspoonfuls of dough in balls about 1 inch in diameter. Place 2 inches apart on greased baking sheets. Dip fingers into granulated sugar to prevent sticking; lightly press balls in rounds 1-1/2 inches in diameter. Press pignolia into tops of cookies. Bake in preheated oven 20 to 25 minutes or until edges are golden brown and tops have browned slightly. Do not overbake. Carefully remove cookies to wire racks and cool. Store several days in a tightly covered container to mellow before serving. Makes 30 to 36 cookies.

TIP To make homemade almond paste, grind 1-1/2 cups whole blanched almonds in a blender or food processor. In a small bowl, combine almonds, 1-1/2 cups powdered sugar, 1 egg white, 1 teaspoon almond extract and 1/8 teaspoon salt. Work to a stiff paste. Refrigerate in an airtight container. Makes 1-1/3 cups.

Paula Pezzi   South Milwaukee, Wisconsin   Wisconsin State Fair

Rosettes

Rosettes are the true test of skill among Scandinavian pastry makers. A perfect deep fat fried rosette has a fresh, delicate flavor, is crisp and so light it threatens to float off the plate. Marjorie Johnson challenged herself to develop a perfect rosette by experimenting with several different recipes. Through trial and error she developed the best proportions of ingredients. Then she kept making them until she learned the techniques that spelled success.

2 eggs, slightly beaten
1 tablespoon sugar
1/4 teaspoon salt
1 teaspoon vanilla extract
1 cup milk
1 tablespoon vegetable oil
About 1-1/4 cups all-purpose flour
Vegetable oil
Powdered sugar

In a large bowl, mix eggs, sugar, salt, vanilla, milk and 1 tablespoon vegetable oil. Add enough flour to make a batter with consistency of thick cream. Batter should be smooth; this may take 1 tablespoon more or less than 1-1/4 cups flour. Pour oil into a deep fat fryer or small deep saucepan to 3 inches deep; heat to 365F (185C). Hold rosette iron in hot fat to heat. Remove iron; shake off excess oil onto paper towels. Dip iron into batter to about 1/16 inch from top of iron. Hold batter-dipped iron in hot oil about 30 seconds or until rosette is light golden brown. Drain on paper towels and slide rosette off iron. Repeat with remaining batter. Fry rosettes one after another without delay to make sure iron stays hot. Cool rosettes and sprinkle with powdered sugar. Makes about 36 rosettes.

Marjorie Johnson   Robbinsdale, Minnesota   Minnesota State Fair

CANDY & SNACKS

Candy making at home is having a modest revival after decades of neglect. With the proliferation of shops selling luxurious chocolates and other confections, we have learned what a difference there is between a really fine product and ordinary candy. Candy makers know that good homemade treats like fudge and divinity have a flavor that matches the most expensive commercial products and are made with as good or even better quality ingredients. Candy making is considered a cooking art, so it can intimidate even those who consider themselves good cooks and bakers. But is it really more difficult to make a batch of candy than to bake and frost a layer cake?

In candy making—as in baking—art is involved, but so is science. Candy making requires following precise rules and recipes. Anyone who can do that can make *good* candy. With a little practice to develop a feeling for working with sugar mixtures, it is not difficult to progress to being a blue-ribbon candy-maker.

These recipes, which spell out the critical steps, give you a chance to try a variety of candies, from easy to challenging. If your interest lies more in making nutritious snacks, you also can discover the secrets of making prize-winning fruit leather, trail mix and dried fruit.

Candy Making Helps

Making candy involves changing sugar and liquid into a syrup and then cooling the syrup which transforms it into candy. Frequently, the cooled syrup is also beaten. This makes it one of the most exacting kinds of cooking. These explanations will help you understand why you need to follow the rules to be successful.

Don't make candy on a humid day. Divinity is the most affected by high humidity, but it also can keep other candy from thickening as it should. When the temperature is above 80F (25C) and the humidity is much above 50 percent, it can effect results. If you have air conditioning in the kitchen, turn it on. Above all, avoid cooking anything that will produce steam at the same time.

Use a thermometer. The kind of candy you get depends on the stage to which the syrup is cooked: soft ball for fudge; hard crack for peanut brittle, for example. The difference between one stage and the next is only a few degrees. The easiest way to gauge this accurately is with a thermometer that measures from 100F (40C) to 400F (205C).

Test the thermometer to see where water boils at your altitude. Then adjust recipes accordingly. For example, if water boils at 210F (99C), subtract two degrees (one degree C) from the recipe temperature. If boiling is 214F (101C), add two degrees (one degree C).

Use the correct size saucepan. Candy mixtures boil up while cooking. If the pan is too small, the mixture will boil over. If the pan is too big, the syrup will cook too fast. It also will be difficult to get an accurate reading on the thermometer if there is not enough liquid to cover the bulb.

Use a heavy pan. The syrup needs to cook at an even, steady rate. It will cook unevenly in a lightweight pan and also may scorch.

Stir with a wooden spoon. A wooden spoon won't heat up in very hot syrup. Also, you can tell by the feel and sound if the sugar crystals are dissolved. You can't do this with a metal spoon.

Dissolve the sugar and liquid before the syrup starts to boil and thicken. If the sugar isn't dissolved at this stage, the candy will be grainier.

Pour candy into a prepared pan. Candy thickens suddenly at the final stage. If you have to stop to butter a pan, you may not get the candy out before it has thickened too much.

If you want to take the candy out in a block, instead of buttering the pan, line it with two strips of foil, using strips long enough to make an overhang on all four sides. Butter the foil. Lift the cooled block of candy out by the extended strips.

Storing Candy

Homemade candy will keep for two to three weeks if you follow these guidelines:

Air is the enemy. Soft candies like divinity and fudge will dry out within an hour. Pralines will dry out almost immediately. Brittles and other candy cooked to a high temperature will get sticky. Gels are the exception. They need to air dry to keep well.

Wrap candy in plastic film. Store it in an airtight container in a cool, dry place. Refrigerate it in hot weather.

Fudge and other candy molded in a pan can be refrigerated in a block. Score the pieces in the pan while the fudge is still warm but don't cut through. Remove the block of candy from the pan, wrap tightly in plastic film, then slip into a plastic bag or wrap in foil. Cut before serving.

Refrigerated candy should be brought to room temperature before unwrapping to prevent discoloration.

Most candy can be frozen for longer storage. One exception is divinity, which may become grainy. Wrapping it to keep out all air is essential. Thaw candy and bring to room temperature before unwrapping.

Store hard and soft candies separately.

Fudge

Illinois loves its fairs. In addition to the big state fair at Springfield, there are more than 50 regional celebrations. By far the biggest of these is the Heart of Illinois Fair in Peoria, which is noted for its culinary department. JoAnne Gudat, who specialty is candy, shares her tips for making old-fashioned creamy, smooth fudge. Before you begin, you will need a good candy thermometer, a sturdy wooden spoon (muscle power is the only choice) and a heavy saucepan. Prepare the pan to mold the fudge in advance. Once the fudge thickens you need to turn it into the pan without any delay. Don't rush any of the steps. Fudge will take about two hours to make, including cooling time.

3 cups sugar
2/3 cup unsweetened cocoa powder
1/8 teaspoon salt
1-1/2 cups milk
1/4 cup butter or margarine
1 teaspoon vanilla extract

Butter an 8- or 9-inch-square pan. In a large heavy saucepan, combine sugar, cocoa powder and salt; stir in milk. Bring to a boil over medium heat, stirring constantly with a wooden spoon to dissolve sugar. Clip thermometer on side of pan, making sure bulb does not rest on bottom of pan. Continue to cook, stirring constantly, to 234F (112C); mixture should boil at a moderate steady rate. Remove from heat. Drop in butter and vanilla but *do not stir*. Cool at room temperature to 110F (44C), about 1 hour. Remove candy thermometer. Beat with a wooden spoon until fudge becomes very thick and loses its gloss. Immediately spread fudge in prepared pan. While it is still warm, score in 1-inch squares. Cool and finish cutting. Makes 64 pieces.

JoAnne Gudat   Edwards, Illinois   Heart of Illinois Fair

Peanut Butter Fudge

If beating fudge by hand for a long time isn't appealing, try this rich Peanut Butter Fudge instead. Marshmallow creme helps give it a creamy, smooth texture without beating. Leah Traxler developed her prize winning Peanut Butter Fudge as a variation of the usual chocolate confection.

4 cups sugar
1-1/3 cups undiluted
   evaporated milk
1/2 cup butter
1 (7-oz.) jar marshmallow creme
1 cup creamy peanut butter
1 cup chopped walnuts
1-1/2 teaspoons vanilla extract
Walnut pieces, if desired

Butter a 13" x 9" baking pan. In a large heavy saucepan, combine sugar, evaporated milk and butter. Cook over medium heat until mixture boils, stirring constantly to dissolve sugar. Clip thermometer on side of pan, making sure bulb does not rest on bottom of pan. Boil, stirring occasionally, to 234F (112C), about 13 to 15 minutes. Syrup should form a ball in cold water which does not retain its shape when taken out of water. Remove from heat; add remaining ingredients. Beat just enough to blend thoroughly. Immediately pour into prepared pan. While candy is warm, score in 1-inch pieces. Sprinkle with walnuts, if desired. Cool and finish cutting. Makes 117 pieces, about 3 pounds.

Leah J. Traxler   Mt. Vernon, Ohio   Ohio State Fair

Kentucky Pralines

Pecan pralines began as a classic Creole candy. The sweet, rich confection was soon adopted through the South, with a surprising number of variations on the basic recipe of sugar, liquid and butter. Kenneth Anderson's Kentucky version uses both brown and granulated sugar plus corn syrup. Instead of the cream many recipes call for, he uses water but adds more butter. The result is a smooth, melt-in-the-mouth confection filled with chunks of pecans. For inexperienced praline makers, the trick is learning that fleeting moment when the candy is thick enough to spoon out before it loses its gloss. However, if you miss that stage the first time, the pralines will still taste delicious.

1 cup sugar
1 cup firmly packed brown sugar
1/4 cup light corn syrup
1/2 cup butter
1/2 cup water
1 cup pecan pieces

In a heavy 2-quart saucepan, combine all ingredients except pecans. Cook over medium heat until syrup boils, stirring constantly with a wooden spoon to dissolve sugars. Clip candy thermometer on side of pan, making sure bulb does not rest on bottom of pan. Cook, stirring occasionally, to 234F (112C). Syrup should form a ball in cold water which does not retain its shape when taken out of water. Remove from heat and cool without stirring to 200F (94C). Remove thermometer, stir in pecans and beat vigorously with a wooden spoon until mixture begins to thicken and change color but is still glossy. Immediately drop by teaspoonfuls onto waxed paper. If candy becomes too stiff, stir in a few drops of hot water. When pralines have set, store tightly covered. Makes about 24 small pralines.

Kenneth Anderson   Louisville, Kentucky   Kentucky State Fair

Classic Divinity

Before the days of heavy-duty home mixers, making divinity required the stong arms of several people in turn. Betty Kerns, a talented candy-maker, confesses that she has burned out several mixer motors over the years as she has made her prize-winning divinity. Since the basic candy recipes are similar, she says beating long enough is the real secret. Because this is such a dense mixture, you must use a heavy, freestanding machine, not a hand mixer. A candy thermometer and heavy saucepan also are necessary. For best results, don't try to make divinity on a humid day.

2-2/3 cups sugar
2/3 cup light corn syrup
1/2 cup water
2 egg whites
1 teaspoon vanilla extract
2/3 cup chopped nuts

In a heavy 2-quart saucepan, combine sugar, corn syrup and water. Cook *just* to boiling, stirring constantly with a wooden spoon to dissolve sugar. Clip candy thermometer on side of pan, making sure bulb does not rest on bottom of pan. *Without stirring*, cook syrup over medium heat to 260F (127C). Remove saucepan from heat. Using a heavy-duty freestanding mixer, immediately beat egg whites until stiff peaks form. Continuing to beat, remove thermometer from saucepan and *slowly* pour a thin stream of hot syrup into egg whites. Syrup will not blend with beaten whites if added too quickly. Add vanilla and continue beating at high speed until mixture becomes slightly dull. Stir in nuts. Drop a spoonful of candy from the tip of a buttered spoon onto wax paper. If it stays in a soft mound, continue spooning out rest of candy. If not, beat a little longer and test again. If mixture becomes too stiff, stir in hot water, a few drops at a time. Makes about 48 pieces.

Betty Kerns   Circleville, Ohio   Ohio State Fair

Divinity (Two-Pan Method)

One of the country's youngest state fair blue ribbon winners in an adult division, Lora Malnaa was getting ready to start her junior year in high school when she received her best of show award for divinity. Already an experienced cook, she used her grandmother's old recipe which calls for making two syrups. One is cooked to the standard hard ball stage and the other to a soft crack stage. Since the candy sets up faster with this method, it probably was developed when divinity had to be beaten by hand. Lora emphasizes that she doesn't stir the syrup once she starts to heat it. This means the mixture must be stirred very well to dissolve the sugar before cooking, rather than as the syrup comes to a boil in a conventional recipe. Two candy thermometers would be helpful, as well as a heavy freestanding mixer.

4 cups sugar
1-1/2 cups water
1 cup light corn syrup
3 egg whites, room temperature
1 teaspoon almond extract
1-1/2 cups chopped pecans, if desired

🏵 Line 2 baking sheets with waxed paper. In a heavy 2-quart saucepan, combine 3 cups of sugar, 3/4 cup of water and corn syrup. Stir mixture with a wooden spoon to dissolve sugar. Clip thermometer on side of pan, making sure bulb does not rest on bottom of pan. Without stirring, cook over medium heat to 260F (127C). Syrup should form a ball in cold water and hold shape out of water. Remove from heat. Meanwhile, while syrup is cooking, in a small saucepan, mix remaining 1 cup of sugar and 3/4 cup of water until sugar dissolves. Cook, without stirring, over medium heat to 275F (135C). Syrup dropped in cold water should form pliable threads. Remove from heat. When first pan of syrup reaches 260F (127C) and is taken off heat, beat egg whites in a large bowl until stiff. Gradually pour a thin stream of first pan of syrup over egg whites, beating at high speed 5 minutes. Scrape sides of bowl occasionally. Immediately add contents of second saucepan in a thin, slow stream, continuing to beat. Add almond extract. Beat until candy forms ripples on surface and starts to lose its gloss. Immediately stop beating and drop a spoonful of candy from outside edge of bowl on baking sheet. If candy does not hold its shape, continue to beat no more than 1 minute and test again. When mound of candy holds its shape, stir in pecans and quickly spoon out remaining divinity onto waxed paper, starting from outside edge of bowl where candy is coolest. Do not scrape sides of bowl; that divinity will be grainy. If mixture gets too stiff before spooning out, stir in hot water, a few drops at a time, until it reaches a spoonable consistency. Makes about 60 pieces.

Lora Malnaa   Minot, North Dakota   North Dakota State Fair

Peanut Brittle

Commercial peanut brittle can't compare with Brenda Danuser's blue ribbon recipe for crisp, rich-flavored candy loaded with peanuts that you can make at home. Use raw peanuts, not salted, and make sure they taste fresh.

1-1/2 cups sugar
1 cup light corn syrup
1 cup water
3 tablespoons margarine
3-1/2 cups raw peanuts (about 1 pound)
1/1/2 teaspoons baking soda
1 teaspoon water
1 teaspoon vanilla extract

Butter a large spoon and jelly-roll pan. Keep jelly-roll pan warm in oven at lowest setting. In a heavy 3-quart saucepan, combine sugar, corn syrup and water. Cook over medium heat to boiling, stirring constantly with a wooden spoon to dissolve sugar. Clip thermometer on side of pan, making sure bulb does not touch bottom of pan. Boil, stirring occasionally, at a steady moderate rate to 240F (116C). Add margarine and peanuts. Continue to cook to 300F (149C). Syrup should form brittle threads in cold water. Remove from heat. Meanwhile, in a small bowl, combine baking soda, water and vanilla. Immediately stir baking soda mixture into syrup; mixture will foam up. Pour onto greased jelly-roll pan. Using buttered spoon, quickly and gently spread candy 1/4-inch thick or thinner if desired. Cool completely, then break candy in pieces. Makes about 2 pounds.

Brenda Danuser   Montreal, Missouri   Missouri State Fair

Cranlets

Reminiscent of Applets, a favorite West Coast apple candy, Cranlets have a slightly tart fruit flavor and a tender, chewy texture. Jan Wagner used a family recipe for this refreshing, unusual candy, which would make an especially attractive addition to a plate of Thanksgiving or Christmas sweets. Make the Cranlets at least three days before serving to give the candy time to firm up and to develop flavor. Then it will keep fresh for weeks in a covered container.

1 (16-oz.) can jellied cranberry sauce
1 cup sugar
2 (3-oz.) packages lemon-flavored gelatin
1 (3-oz.) package orange-flavored gelatin
1-1/2 cups coarsely chopped walnuts
3/4 cup sugar

In a medium-size saucepan, melt cranberry sauce over low heat, stirring frequently. Remove from heat. Stir in 1 cup of sugar and gelatins. Return to heat. Bring mixture to a boil, stirring constantly. Remove from heat. Stir in walnuts. Pour into an 8-inch-square metal baking pan. Refrigerate overnight on a level surface. Line a box or large pan with waxed paper. Cut candy in 1-inch-square pieces. Roll in 3/4 cup sugar. Arrange candy pieces in box, using waxed paper between layers. Cover and store at room temperature at least 3 days before serving. Candy will keep for several weeks. Makes about 80 pieces.

Jan Wagner   Salem, Oregon   Oregon State Fair

Caramel Corn

Robin Tarbell carries on a family tradition when she brings home a multitude of blue ribbons from the state fair. Between them, her mother and her grandmother accumulated more than 6,000 ribbons before they both retired from competition several years ago. Iowa's reputation as the corn state includes raising popcorn. The young legal secretary won a case of popcorn as well as a blue ribbon for her deluxe version of caramel corn which includes pecan halves and burnt sugar flavoring. If you can't locate this specialty flavoring, the candy will still be delicious without it.

8 quarts popped corn
1 cup pecan halves
2 cups brown sugar
1 cup margarine
1/2 cup light corn syrup
1/2 teaspoon salt
1 teaspoon vanilla extract
1 teaspoon burnt sugar flavoring
1/2 teaspoon baking soda

Grease 2 large baking pans. Remove any unpopped kernels from popped corn. Keep popcorn and pecans warm in a 250F (120C) oven while making caramel mixture. In a heavy 4-quart saucepan, combine brown sugar, margarine, corn syrup, salt and flavorings. Bring to a boil, stirring constantly with a wooden spoon to dissolve sugar. Boil 3 minutes, stirring occasionally. Mix in baking soda thoroughly. Place popped corn and pecans in a large bowl. Pour caramel over popped corn and pecans, stirring gently to coat popped kernels. Spoon caramel corn into greased baking pans. Bake in 250F (120C) oven 40 to 60 minutes or until crisp, stirring every 15 minutes. Turn caramel corn out onto sheets of foil. Cool completely, then break in pieces. Store in tightly covered containers. Makes about 8-1/2 quarts.

Robin Tarbell   Centerville, Iowa   Iowa State Fair

Orange Balls

Winner of the prestigious Ozark Empire Cookie Jar award, Margo Shull arranged a selection of five different kinds of cookies made from a variety of doughs in a clear container. The exhibit was judged on the appearance of the container as well as the quality of the contents. Her selection included this unbaked confection that could pass either as a cookie or candy. Orange Balls should be made several days before serving to allow the flavor to develop. These will keep well for several weeks in a tightly-covered container.

1 (12-oz.) package vanilla wafers, finely crushed
1 cup ground pecans
2 cups powdered sugar
1 (6-oz.) can frozen orange-juice concentrate, thawed
1/2 cup margarine, melted
1 to 1-1/4 cups flaked coconut

In a large bowl, combine vanilla wafer crumbs, pecans and powdered sugar. Add orange-juice concentrate and margarine, stirring until very well blended. Let stand 5 minutes to absorb liquid. Form level tablespoonfuls of dough in balls. Roll in coconut. For best flavor, store in a covered container in a cool place for several days before serving. Makes 48 balls.

Margo J. Shull   Springfield, Missouri   Ozark Empire Fair

Pineapple-Apricot Leather

Fruit leathers, translucent sheets of dried fruit puree, can be sun-dried in California's hot summer sun, where Marilyn Martell creates prize winning variations of the nutritious snack. In less sunner or more humid climates, the thin sheets can be dried in a very low oven, although sun-dried fruit has a better texture. Some leather-makers dry the fruit puree on sheets of plastic, but she has found this can affect the flavor. She recommends instead using shallow nonstick baking pans.

1 (20-oz.) can juice-packed crushed pineapple
2 cups drained home canned apricot halves
or 1-1/2 (17-oz.) cans apricot halves, drained

Lightly oil 2 (15″ x 12″) nonstick baking pans with edges on all sides. In a blender, process fruit at high speed 2 to 3 minutes or until smooth. Pour 1/2 of fruit puree into each pan and spread to cover evenly. Sun dry on a smooth level surface in full hot sun up to 24 hours; bring inside at night. Or preheat oven to 130F (55C). Dry in preheated oven 6 to 8 hours or until leather does not stick to pan. Place a hot pad in oven door to allow a small opening for steam to escape. Or oven dry 2 hours, then finish in hot sun. When fruit is firm to touch, try peeling it off pan while hot. When whole sheet can be pulled off, it is dry. For best quality leather, do not overdry. Hang dried leather indoors, uncovered, several days. Cut each sheet in 3 pieces. Roll each piece in plastic wrap and seal tightly. Store in an airtight jar at room temperature up to 1 month; refrigerate up to 4 months or freeze for longer storage. Cut in 6 (15″ x 4″) strips. Makes 6 strips.

Marilyn Martell   Reedley, California   California State Fair

Sandy's Trail Mix

In states where camping and hiking are popular activities, state fair contestants vie to see who can develop the best tasting trail mix. Sandy Hansen knows that eye appeal wins extra points, too. So she dries her own fruit or selects the best looking she can find and cuts it in uniformly sized pieces. By putting in a combination of ingredients her family likes best, she has developed her own delicious, healthful snack food.

1/2 cup (1/2-inch-pieces) dried apples
1/2 cup (1/2-inch-pieces) dried apricots
1/2 cup (1/2-inch-pieces) dried pears
1/2 cup (1/2-inch-pieces) dried pineapple
1/2 cup dried bananas
1/2 cup slivered almonds
1/2 cup coconut flakes
1/2 cup raisins
1/2 cup sunflower seeds

In a large bowl, combine all ingredients well. Store in an airtight container. Makes 4-1/2 cups.

Sandy Hansen   Aurora, Colorado   Colorado State Fair

Dried Bananas

French major Traci Durrell's food interests range from studying French cuisine and wines while spending a year in France to being the high-scoring exhibitor in the dried foods division at the Oregon State Fair all four years she has entered there. The former 4-H member recommends drying bananas as a way to use a food dehydrator year round. She chooses large fruit that is ripe enough for good flavor, but firm enough to cut in very thin slices. When selecting slices for fair competition, her championship advice is to pick the pieces that are largest in diameter, uniformly round and thin and with a natural creamy color. Dried bananas make a nutritious snack and are easy to carry for bag lunches as well as for backpack meals.

2 large medium-ripe bananas for each 14-inch-square
food dehydrator tray

Set food dehydrator at 135F (55C). Peel bananas; cut in very thin 1/16-inch slices, making straight even slices that are round, not elongated. Arrange slices on dehydrator tray. As each tray is filled, immediately place tray in dehydrator to minimize darkening. Dry 8 to 10 hours, depending on ripeness of fruit, humidity and temperature. Turn trays a half turn every 2 to 3 hours for more even drying. To test slices for dryness, cool 5 to 10 minutes. Surface should not feel sticky and no moisture should appear when a slice is broken in half. Freeze dried bananas in tightly-closed plastic bags. One banana makes about 1/2 cup.

Traci Durrell   Philomath, Oregon   Oregon State Fair

SWEET SPREADS

Americans are rediscovering the joys of growing vegetables and fruit, then putting up the harvest. Just as gardening often is a hobby rather than a necessity, recreational food preservation—making fancy preserves—is outstripping the more utilitarian canning of fruits and vegetables that earlier generations needed to supplement their limited winter diets.

Both men and women are preserving and discovering the satisfaction of turning out their own specialities that are even better than the expensive products in food stores.

Mastering the ancient art of preserving and experiencing the pleasure of putting a little of summer into jars is a growing trend. Nowhere does it show up more clearly than in the expanding number of exhibits and exhibitors at America's largest state and regional fairs.

Blue Ribbon Advice for Fair Exhibitors

Write to the fair office well in advance for a premium book. It will list its specific rules for exhibiting preserved food, such as size and kind of jars and lids allowed, methods of processing and labels. Any product that doesn't conform will be disqualified.

Many premium books also tell how products are judged and scored. Learn in advance what counts.

Preserved food can never be better than the ingredients. Use the freshest, best quality fruits and vegetables available at the optimum stage of ripeness for your product.

Beautiful but flavorless fruit, slightly stale nuts or old spices will count against you. Taste your ingredients before you go to the work of putting them up.

Color, texture and overall appearance can determine nearly two-thirds of the score in some products. Make yours look as good as possible.

Hide the jars you plan to exhibit so no one uses them by mistake.

Store your preserving in a cool dry, dark place for best color and quality. This is good advice for all canning, not just exhibit jars.

Don't attempt preserving when you are feeling rushed. It can't be hurried, so relax and enjoy doing it.

When you are in the middle of preserving, let the phone ring.

Preventing Fruit from Darkening

Some light-colored fruits will darken when peeled or cut. In recipes where fresh, bright color is important, the following need to be treated in Acidulated Water Solution or with a commercial antioxidant: apples, apricots, nectarines, peaches and pears. Some varieties of these fruits are more susceptible to browning than others.

Acidulated Water Solution

The easiest and least expensive treatment is to make your own acidulated water solution by mixing 2 tablespoons salt and 2 tablespoons vinegar in 1 gallon water. Peel or slice fruit directly into this solution.

Antioxidant Solution

Two types of these antidarkening agents can be purchased: a commercial antioxidant sold in food stores or a powdered form of vitamin C (ascorbic acid), available in drug or health food stores. When using either of these products, follow package directions.

Taking the Mystery Out of Making Preserves and Jelly

Preserves are a mixture of fruit heated with sugar, which includes pectin and acid for good consistency and flavor. Whether the sweet spread is called jam, preserves, marmalade, conserve, fruit butter or honey depends on the complexity of ingredients, size of the cooked fruit and consistency of the finished product.

Jellies are a combination of fruit juice, pectin, sugar and acid in critical proportions to make a clear, sparkling gel that holds its shape, yet is tender.

You will notice from the recipes in this book that even experienced jelly and jam makers add commercial pectin to get their blue ribbons. Commercial pectins produce more predictable results, but it is essential to follow exact directions.

Other kinds of preserves made without added pectin allow for somewhat more creativity, as long as basic proportions of ingredients and proper cooking times are observed.

Rule #1 is to read the recipe in advance. While only a few of these recipes call for a two-day process, once you begin to cook a batch of jelly or preserves, often you can't stop without ruining it. Some ingredients may need advance preparation; everything should be measured out, ready to add, and equipment must be ready to use.

Rule #2 is don't try to double the recipe. It probably won't work.

Like making candy and some frostings, you'll have more success if you can avoid cooking these high-sugar spreads on a hot, humid day. Some prize-winning preservers report that they always turn on the air conditioner before they begin.

How Can I Tell When My Jelly and Preserves Are Done?

Experienced preservers can simply glance at the bubbles on boiling jelly or note the way preserves feel on the stirring spoon and know that they are nearly ready for the jars. But anyone who makes jellies and jams only occasionally needs measurable guidelines.

When making **jelly** and the recipe calls for added pectin, use only the kind specified and follow directions exactly. If you haven't used pectin, the most accurate test is to use a thermometer. Cook until the temperature at sea level reaches 220F (105C). (Find the correct temperature by determining the temperature at which water boils, then adding eight degrees to get the jelling point.)

Lacking a thermometer, use the less accurate *sheeting test*: dip a cold metal spoon into the boiling jelly and watch how the mixture runs off the side of the spoon. When it is almost ready, it will slowly come together and fall off the spoon in two drops. At the correct jelling point, it will slide off the spoon in a sheet. You will need several clean, cold spoons to carry out this test.

Jams, preserves, conserve and butter should be less firm than jelly, and cooking is not quite as critical. If commercial pectin is used, follow directions. If not, recipe cooking times, which can only be approximate, plus a thermometer (to about 218F/103C at sea level) will produce a product that spreads easily, is tender and mounds up on a spoon.

Lacking a thermometer, the *plate test*, is reasonably accurate. Place a spoonful of the hot fruit mixture on a chilled plate. Put the plate in the freezer one minute. If there is no watery ring around the mound, draw your finger through the mixture. It should retain its shape and not flow back through the trough your finger has made.

Recipe Yields

Even if you measure fruits and vegetables by weight, the most accurate way, preserving recipes will have more variables than baking recipes. So many preserving recipes give the yield as a range. The easy solution: just prepare an extra jar for any "bonus".

Water-Bath Canner

Preserving recipes in this book, except for jelly, call for processing in a water-bath canner. (Many older recipes eliminate this step.) This is to make sure that bacteria, enzymes, yeasts and molds that can cause problems are destroyed.

This process often is referred to as a *boiling* water bath, which can be confusing, since research shows that sweet preserves can be processed at *simmering* water temperatures (about 180F/80C) for the time recommended in the recipe.

Canned fruit, tomato products, condiments and some pickles and relishes, on the other hand, do need to be processed in boiling water (212F/95C) to prevent spoilage.

A few state fairs require that jelly for exhibiting be processed five minutes in a simmering water bath. Since this may break down jelly made with added commercial pectin, most food scientists feel that under ordinary circumstances, pouring the hot jelly into sterilized jars and using sterilized two-part lids is all that is needed.

Ingredients

All blue ribbon winners strongly emphasize using quality ingredients, with fruit at the ideal stage of ripeness for the recipe. Many raise their own or buy from local growers.

Equipment

A novice jelly maker can have a moment of sheer panic the first time a few cups of juice and sugar begin to boil up and overflow a saucepan. A big preserving kettle—six- to eight-quarts—is essential. Use unchipped enamelware, stainless steel or heavy aluminum.

A timer that can be set for exactly one minute or a clock or watch with a minute hand is necessary for jellies and jam made with commercial pectin.

For other preserves, a candy or fat thermometer will tell you most accurately when the mixture is ready to go into the jars.

If you plan to extract juice from fruit to make jelly, you will need a jelly bag or large sieve or colander lined with cheese-cloth.

Canning Jars

For exhibiting at most fairs and for home use, standard half-pint or pint canning jars and two-piece lids are best, since water bath processing is recommended for all sweet spreads except jelly.

For short storage—six months or less—sterilized jelly jars sealed with paraffin can be used, particularly in a cool, dry climate. Should mold develop, discard the preserves.

Chokecherry Jelly

A small, black cherry that grows wild in many parts of the country, chokecherries are too astringent to be eaten as fruit, but they make a wonderful dark, rich-flavored jelly. Janelle Reff discovered a first-time novice jelly-maker could compete with the experts when she won a blue ribbon with this recipe.

4 pounds ripe (black) chokecherries, stems removed, washed, drained
2-1/2 cups water
1 (1-3/4-oz.) box powdered pectin
4-1/2 cups sugar

To make juice, in a large kettle, crush fruit with a potato masher. Add water, bring to a boil. Cover and simmer on medium heat 25 minutes, stirring occasionally, continuing to crush fruit. Dampen a jellybag. Pour fruit and liquid into jelly bag. Let juice drip into a large bowl, squeezing bag gently. Sterilize 6 (1/2-pint) jars. Keep hot until needed. Prepare lids as manufacturer directs. Measure 3-1/2 cups juice. In a large kettle, combine juice and pectin. Bring to a boil over high heat, stirring constantly. Add sugar all at once. Cook until mixture comes to a full rolling boil that cannot be stirred down, stirring constantly. Boil exactly 1 minute, stirring constantly. Remove from heat. Quickly skim off foam with a metal spoon. Pour jelly into hot jars, leaving 1/4-inch headspace. Wipe jar rims; seal with hot lids and screw bands. Invert jar 30 seconds, then stand upright to seal. Makes about 6 (1/2-pint) jars.

Janelle Reff Hudson, South Dakota   South Dakota State Fair

Juneberry Jelly

The Juneberry is a native American shrub that grows wild over much of the country. If you are lucky enough to know where to find the bluish-black berries when they ripen in late May or June, you can duplicate this beautiful deep-red jelly that brought Louise Schneiderman one of her 74 ribbons from the 1986 state fair.

3 quarts mostly ripe Juneberries, stems removed, washed, drained
1 cup water
2 tablespoons lemon juice
1 (1-3/4-oz.) box powdered pectin
5 cups sugar

To make juice, pour berries into a large kettle; crush to help extract juice. Add water. Heat to boiling; simmer about 10 minutes, stirring often to prevent scorching. Cool. Pour fruit and juice into a muslin bag; let juice drip into a large bowl. For clearest juice, do not squeeze bag. Discard fruit. Juice can be used immediately, refrigerated 1 to 2 days or frozen for later use. Sterilize 6 (1/2-pint) jars. Keep hot until needed. Prepare lids as manufacturer directs. In a large kettle, combine Juneberry juice, lemon juice and pectin. Bring to a full rolling boil, stirring constantly. Add sugar; continue to stir until mixture returns to a full rolling boil. Boil exactly 1 minute. Remove from heat. Skim off foam with a metal spoon. Pour jelly into hot jars, leaving 1/8-inch headspace. Wipe jar rims; seal with hot lids and screw bands. Invert jars 30 seconds, then stand upright to cool. Makes 6 (1/2-pint) jars.

Louise Schneiderman   Bottineau, N. Dakota   N. Dakota State Fair

Fresh Mint Jelly

Eunice Leach started entering her jellies at the state fair three years ago, after she had retired from teaching. She immediately began to win ribbons and now has a small business selling her preserves. If you use homegrown mint, as she does, pick it just before the flower buds open for maximum flavor.

1-1/2 cups packed mint leaves, crushed
3-1/4 cups water
2 to 3 drops green food coloring
1 (1-3/4-oz.) box powdered fruit pectin
4 cups sugar

Sterilize 6 (1/2-pint) jars. Keep hot until needed. Prepare lids as manufacturer directs. In a medium-size saucepan, combine mint leaves and water. Bring mixture to a boil. Remove from heat, cover and let stand 10 minutes. Strain; measure 3 cups of mint infusion. Add food coloring to tint light green. In a large kettle, mix mint infusion and pectin. Stir until pectin dissolves. Increase heat to high. Bring mixture to a boil, stirring constantly. Add sugar all at once. Cook and stir as mixture comes to a rolling boil that cannot be stirred down. Boil exactly 1 minute, stirring constantly. Remove from heat. Quickly skim off foam with a metal spoon. Pour jelly into hot jars, leaving 1/8-inch headspace. Wipe jar rim; seal with hot lids and screw bands. Invert jar 30 seconds, then stand upright to cool. Makes 6 (1/2-pint) jars.

Eunice R. Leach   Wendell, North Carolina   North Carolina State Fair

Spiced Plum Jelly

Competing at the Los Angeles County Fair is a family affair for the Roberts. Judi, husband Frank and his mother have been winning ribbons for canning and baking for nearly a decade. Now their young daughters are bringing home ribbons in the Junior Fair category. For her jelly, Judi Roberts picks plums that are juicy-ripe but without skin breaks from a backyard tree.

> *4 pounds red plums, washed*
> *1 cup water*
> *4 whole cloves*
> *2 (3-inch) cinnamon sticks*
> *6-1/2 cups sugar*
> *1 (3-oz.) pouch liquid pectin*

To make juice, in a large kettle, place plums, water and spices. Cover and simmer over medium heat about 10 minutes or until pulp separates from pits. Discard spices; pour juice through a jelly bag or cheesecloth-lined sieve. Let juice drip into a large bowl without squeezing pulp. For very clear jelly, refrigerate juice overnight to allow sediment to settle. Sterilize 7 (1/2-pint) jars. Keep hot until needed. Prepare lids as manufacturer directs. Measure 4 cups clear juice. In a large kettle, mix juice and sugar. Bring to a boil over high heat, stirring constantly. Stir in liquid pectin. Bring mixture to a full rolling boil; boil hard exactly 1 minute, stirring constantly. Remove from heat. Skim off foam with a metal spoon. Immediately ladle into hot jars, leaving 1/8-inch headspace. Wipe jar rims; seal with hot lids and screw bands. Invert jar 30 seconds, then stand upright to seal. Makes 7 (1/2-pint) jars.

Judi Roberts   Claremont, California   Los Angeles County Fair

Downeast Fruit Jelly

Originally from Maine, Carla Bouffard combined a Downeasters' practicality with her own creativity to develop what must be one of the simplest recipes ever to capture a sweepstakes award for jellies. The combination of apple, grape and raspberry reminded her of fruit she could pick in Maine, hence the name.

3 cups bottled blend of apple, grape and raspberry juice
1 (1-3/4-oz.) box powdered pectin
4 cups sugar

Sterilize 5 (1/2-pint) jars. Keep hot until needed. Prepare lids as manufacturer directs. In a large kettle, combine juice and pectin. Bring to a boil over high heat, stirring constantly. Add sugar; mix well. Bring to a full, rolling boil that cannot be stirred down, stirring constantly. Boil hard exactly 2 minutes. Remove from heat. Skim off foam with a metal spoon. Immediately ladle into hot jars, leaving 1/4-inch headspace. Wipe jar rims; seal with hot lids and screw bands. Invert jar 30 seconds, then stand upright to seal. Makes about 5 (1/2-pint) jars.

TIP Other blends of fruit juice can be substituted, if desired.

Carla Bouffard   Salina, Kansas   Kansas State Fair

Double Hot Pepper Jelly

Vandy Bradow admits she has a high tolerance for fiery food, so she uses two varieties of hot peppers to make her jelly instead of a combination of sweet and hot peppers. She often serves her attractive red and green pepper jelly in the traditional Southern way, spreading it over cream cheese on wheat crackers.

1/4 cup finely-minced red chili pepper
3/4 cup finely-minced green jalapeno peppers
6-1/2 cups sugar
1-1/2 cups distilled white vinegar
2 (3-oz.) pouches liquid pectin

Sterilize 8 (1/2-pint) jars. Keep hot until needed. Prepare lids as manufacturer directs. In a large kettle, combine minced peppers, sugar and vinegar. Bring to a boil. Remove from heat; let stand 5 minutes. Using a metal spoon, skim off any foam. Increase heat to high. Return kettle to heat and bring back to a full rolling boil that cannot be stirred down. Stir in pectin and boil exactly 1 minute, stirring constantly. Remove from heat. Ladle into hot jars, leaving 1/8-inch headspace. Wipe jar rims and seal with hot lids and screw bands. Invert jar 30 seconds, then stand upright to seal. Makes about 8 (1/2-pint) jars.

VARIATION   For a less assertive flavor, substitute sweet bell peppers for part of hot peppers.

TIP   *Wear rubber or plastic gloves while cutting hot peppers and do not touch skin or eyes.* To mince peppers, using a sharp knife, cut off tops and slice lengthwise. Discard seeds and white membrane. Cut lengthwise in 1/8-inch strips, then cut very fine crosswise strips.

Vandy Bradow   Raleigh, North Carolina   North Carolina State Fair

Dewberry (Blackberry) Jam

Southern cooks are more likely to use dewberries, while northerners pick blackberries to make the same delectable jam. Jacqueline Jones chops the berries in her food processor and removes some of the seeds to get her blue ribbon product.

3 quarts dewberries or blackberries
1 (1-3/4-oz.) box powdered pectin
7 cups sugar

Thoroughly wash and scald 4 (1-pint) jars. Keep hot until needed. Prepare lids as manufacturer directs. Wash berries and drain thoroughly. Chop berries in a food processor or crush with a potato masher. Push 1/2 of pulp through a sieve to remove seeds. Measure 5 cups prepared pulp. In a large kettle, combine pulp and pectin. Bring to a full rolling boil over high heat, stirring constantly. Add sugar all at once. Continuing to stir, bring mixture back to a boil and boil hard exactly 1 minute. Remove from heat. Skim off foam with a metal spoon. Ladle into hot jars, leaving 1/4-inch headspace. Wipe jar rims; seal with hot lids and screw bands. Process 15 minutes in a simmering water bath. Makes about 4 (1-pint) jars.

Jacqueline Jones   Boyce, Louisiana   Louisiana State Fair

Blue Ribbon Raspberry Jam

Evelyn Chinick picks raspberries from her own bushes to make jam with a lovely fresh flavor. She combines equal amounts of uncooked juice and crushed berries.

3 cups raspberry juice
3 cups crushed fully ripe raspberries
1 (1-3/4-oz.) box powdered pectin
8-1/2 cups sugar

Sterilize 8 (1/2-pint) jars. Keep hot until needed. Prepare lids as manufacturer directs. In a large kettle, combine raspberry juice, crushed fruit and powdered pectin., stirring until dissolved. Bring to a full rolling boil over high heat, stirring constantly. Add sugar, stirring constantly, and bring back to a boil that cannot be stirred down. Boil exactly 1 minute. Remove from heat. Skim off foam with a metal spoon. Immediately ladle into hot jars, leaving 1/4-inch headspace. Wipe jar rims; seal with hot lids and screw bands. Invert jars 30 seconds, then stand upright to cool. Makes about 8 (1/2-pint) jars.

VARIATION To make an intensely-flavored raspberry juice, squeeze enough crushed berries through a jelly bag made from 2 layers muslin to make 3 cups juice. Refrigerate juice several hours and ladle off clear juice.

Evelyn Chinick Mountlake Terrace, Washington   Washington State Fair

Plum Jam

Harvey Canady turned cooking as a hobby into a small home business, filling requests from friends who wanted to order his specialties. Any slightly-tart, flavorful plum can be used to make his colorful jam, which has won blue ribbons for the last five years.

4 pounds plums, washed
1/2 cup water
8 cups sugar
1 (1-3/4-oz.) box powdered pectin

Thoroughly wash and scald 6 (1/2-pint) jars. Keep hot until needed. Prepare lids as manufacturer directs. Pit (do not peel) plums. Finely chop fruit or grind in a food chopper; measure 6 cups. In a large kettle, combine plums and water. Cover and simmer 5 minutes, stirring occasionally. Stir pectin into fruit mixture. Bring to a full boil over high heat, stirring constantly. Stir in sugar. Bring to a full rolling boil; boil 1-1/2 minutes, stirring constantly. Remove from heat. Skim off foam with a large metal spoon. Immediately ladle into hot jars, leaving 1/4-inch headspace. Wipe jar rims; seal jars with hot lids and screw bands. Process 10 minutes in a simmering water bath. Makes 5 to 6 (1/2-pint) jars.

Harvey Canady   Fayetteville, N. Carolina   N. Carolina State Fair

Concord Grape Jam

Since she enters preserving in several county fairs as well as the state fair, Gwendolyn Swenson has an off limits storage area, so her family doesn't use the jars she plans to exhibit. Aromatic home grown grapes, picked at the peak of ripeness, give her jam its winning flavor.

4 pounds Concord grapes
3 cups water
1 (1-3/4-oz.) box powdered pectin
7-1/2 cups sugar

Thoroughly wash and scald 6 (1/2-pint) jars. Keep hot until needed. Prepare lids as manufacturer directs. Wash grapes in cool water, drain and remove stems. In a large kettle, bring grapes and 2 cups of water to a boil over high heat. Cover and simmer about 5 minutes or until grapes are tender, stirring occasionally. Remove from heat. Put through a food mill to remove seeds and skins. Discard seeds and skins. Measure 5 cups of puree. Wash kettle. In washed kettle, combine puree, remaining 1 cup of water and pectin. Bring to a full rolling boil over high heat, stirring constantly. Stir in sugar all at once. Bring back to a full boil and boil hard exactly 1 minute, stirring constantly. Remove from heat. Skim off foam with a metal spoon. Immediately ladle into hot jars, leaving 1/4-inch headspace. Wipe jar rims; seal with hot lids and screw bands. Process 10 minutes in a simmering water bath. Makes about 6 (1/2-pint) jars.

Gwendolyn Swenson   North Branch, Minnesota   Minnesota State Fair

Tart-Sweet Gooseberry Jam

By using plump, ripe gooseberries and a jelling mix, Dawn Squires developed a flavorful jam which calls for about half the usual amount of sugar. *Do not substitute regular powdered pectin.*

4 cups ripe gooseberries, stems and blossom ends removed
Water
1 (2-oz) package jelling mix
2 cups sugar

Wash gooseberries and drain. Pour into a large kettle. Add enough water to barely cover. Bring to a boil; reduce heat and simmer, uncovered, 1 hour, stirring occasionally. Thoroughly wash and scald 5 (1/2-pint) jars. Keep hot until needed. Prepare lids as manufacturer directs. In a blender or food processor, process 1/2 cup liquid from gooseberries, jelling mix and sugar about 30 seconds or until thoroughly combined. Stir into cooked gooseberries. Bring mixture to a rolling boil over high heat, stirring constantly. Boil exactly 2 minutes. Remove from heat. Skim off foam. Ladle jam into hot jars, leaving 1/4-inch head space. Wipe jar rims; seal with hot lids and screw bands. Process 10 minutes in a simmering water bath. Makes 4 to 5 (1/2-pint) jars.

TIP To preserve color, store in a cool dark place and use within 6 months. Refrigerate jam after opening.

Dawn C. Squires   Lodi, California   California State Fair

Door County Cherry Jam

Scenic Door County claims 700,000 trees that produce the sour red cherries for which this northern Wisconsin peninsula is famous. Diane Curley picks her own tree-ripe cherries there every year and immediately processes them into her own special jam.

3-1/2 cups pitted chopped sour cherries
4-1/2 cups sugar
1/2 cup Amaretto
1 (3-oz.) pouch liquid pectin

Thoroughly wash and scald 6 (1/2-pint) jars. Keep hot until needed. Prepare lids as manufacturer directs. In a large kettle, combine cherries, sugar and Amaretto. Bring fruit mixture to a full rolling boil over high heat that cannot be stirred down, stirring constantly. Continuing to stir, boil hard exactly 1 minute. Remove from heat. Stir in liquid pectin. Skim off foam with a metal spoon. Immediately ladle into hot jars, leaving 1/4-inch headspace. Wipe jar rims and seal with hot lids and screw bands. Process 10 minutes in a simmering water bath. Makes 5 to 6 (1/2-pint) jars.

VARIATION Substitute whole cherries frozen without syrup if fresh sour cherries are not available.

Diane Curley   River Hills, Wisconsin   Wisconsin State Fair

Apple Butter

Prize apple butter starts with fruit that quickly becomes soft and mushy when cooked. Depending on the tartness of the apples, you may want to add a bit more or less sugar than Betsy Byrd's old family recipe calls for.

20 *medium-size cooking apples, washed, peeled, cored, sliced*
  (about 5 lbs.)
1 *cup water*
4 *cups granulated sugar*
1/2 *cup light-brown sugar*
1 *teaspoon grated orange peel*
1/3 *cup orange juice*
1/2 *teaspoon ground nutmeg*
1/8 *teaspoon ground ginger*

In a large heavy kettle, combine apples and water. Cover and cook over medium-low heat 30 minutes or until apples are soft, stirring occasionally. Meanwhile, thoroughly wash and scald 5 (1-pint) jars or 10 (1/2-pint) jars. Keep hot until needed. Prepare lids as manufacturer directs. Puree apple mixture in a food processor or food mill. Drain off any liquid. Measure 8 cups puree. Wash kettle. In washed kettle, combine puree, sugars, orange peel and juice, nutmeg and ginger. Cook over medium heat about 15 minutes or until mixture thickens, stirring frequently. Skim off any foam. Ladle into hot jars, leaving 1/4-inch head space. Remove air bubbles by running a table knife inside edge of jar. Wipe jar rims; seal with hot lids and screw bands. Process 10 minutes in a simmering water bath. Makes 5 (1-pint) jars or 10 (1/2-pint) jars.

Betsy Byrd   Raleigh, North Carolina   North Carolina State Fair

Double Apple Butter

Jan Grizel does so much pickling and canning in her mountain home east of Los Angeles that her husband, Don, built an earthquake-proof closet that holds hundreds of jars. Special preserves, like this spicy, not-too-sweet apple butter, are shared in Christmas gift packs.

6 pounds Rome Beauty apples,
    washed, cut in quarters
4 cups apple cider
2-1/2 cups sugar
1 teaspoon ground cinnamon
1/2 teaspoon ground nutmeg
1/4 teaspoon ground cloves
1/4 teaspoon salt

In a large heavy kettle, heat apples and cider over high heat to boiling. Reduce heat to medium. Cover and cook about 20 minutes or until apples are very tender, stirring occasionally. Remove from heat. Press apple mixture through a food mill or coarse sieve into a very large bowl. Discard peels and seeds. Return apple mixture to kettle. Add sugar, cinnamon, nutmeg, cloves and salt. Heat to boiling over high heat. Reduce heat to medium. Cook 1-1/4 hours or until mixture is thickened and mounds when dropped from a spoon, stirring frequently. Meanwhile, thoroughly wash and scald 11 (1/2-pint) jars. Keep hot until needed. Prepare lids as manufacturer directs. Ladle butter into hot jars, leaving 1/4-inch headspace. Remove air bubbles by running a table knife inside edge of jar. Wipe jar rims; seal with hot lids and screw bands. Process 10 minutes in a simmering water bath. Makes about 11 (1/2-pint) jars.

Jan Grizel Forest Falls, California   Los Angeles County Fair

Cranberry-Pear Butter

Make this smooth, bright-flavored spread in the fall when fresh cranberries are available or freeze a few bags to combine with summer pears. Karla Dellner was awarded best of class against all first place fruit butters for her Cranberry Pear Butter.

5 pounds firm-ripe pears, peeled, cored, cut in chunks
4 cups fresh or frozen cranberries
Grated peel 1 lemon
2 tablespoons lemon juice
3 cups cranberry juice
3 cups sugar
1-1/2 teaspoons ground cinnamon
3/4 teaspoon allspice
1/4 teaspoon ground nutmeg

In a large kettle, combine pears, cranberries, lemon peel and juice and cranberry juice. Cover and simmer over medium heat about 30 minutes or until pears and cranberries are soft. Puree fruit mixture in a food mill or press through a sieve. Wash kettle. In washed kettle, combine puree, sugar, cinnamon, allspice and nutmeg. Cook at a slow boil 30 to 45 minutes or until thick, stirring often. Meanwhile, thoroughly wash and scald 4 (1-pint) jars. Keep hot until needed. Prepare lids as manufacturer directs. Remove butter from heat. Ladle into hot jars, leaving 1/4-inch headspace. Wipe jar rims; seal with hot lids and screw bands. Process 15 minutes in a simmering water bath. Makes 3 to 4 (1-pint) jars.

Karla Dellner   Cameron Park, California   California State Fair

Purely Peach Butter

Susan and Harvey Moser used to enjoy visiting competitive exhibits at county and state fairs and telling each other they could do even better. With 318 ribbons between them from exhibits at four fairs this year, few could disagree. Her care in preparing the fruit for peach butter helps explain why it looked, as well as tasted, like a blue ribbon winner to state fair judges.

18 medium-size fully-ripe Elberta peaches
1 gallon Acidulated Water Solution, page 178
Water
4 cups sugar
4 tablespoons lemon juice

One at a time, peel peaches and cut in half. Pit and scrape out red fibers with a spoon. Immediately drop into Acidulated Water Solution to prevent browning. Rinse, drain peaches and chop. In a large kettle, cover chopped fruit with just enough water to prevent scorching. Bring to a boil over medium heat. Reduce heat to low. Cover and cook about 20 minutes or until peaches are tender, stiring occasionally. Puree cooked peaches in a food mill or blender. Rinse kettle. Measure 2 quarts puree into kettle. Mix with sugar and lemon juice. Cook over medium-low heat, stirring frequently, about 30 minutes or until thick and peach butter holds shape while rounding up on a spoon. Meanwhile, thoroughly wash and scald 4 (1-pint) jars. Keep hot until needed. Prepare lids as manufacturer directs. Remove butter from heat. Immediately ladle into hot jars, leaving 1/4-inch headspace. Wipe jar rims; seal with hot lids and screw bands. Process 10 minutes in a simmering water bath. Makes about 4 (1-pint) jars.

Susan C. Moser   King, North Carolina   North Carolina State Fair

Grandma's Fig Preserves

Ripe figs deteriorate quickly and should be processed immediately after picking. Discard any that are cracked. Dorothy Glover's prize recipe calls for long, slow cooking, so a heavy kettle is essential. This two-step method of letting figs stand in syrup overnight plumps up the fruit.

> 6 cups sugar
> 2 cups water
> 2 quarts firm ripe figs, washed (about 4-1/2 lbs.)
> 1 medium-size lemon, thinly sliced

In a large heavy kettle, combine sugar and water. Bring to a boil, stirring frequently to dissolve sugar. Add figs and lemon. Reduce heat; cook, uncovered, at a gentle boil 1 to 1-1/2 hours or until figs are clear and syrup is consistency of honey. Shake kettle occasionally during cooking to prevent sticking, but do not stir. Cover and let fig preserves stand in a cool place overnight. Thoroughly wash and scald 5 (1-pint) jars. Keep hot until needed. Prepare lids as manufacturer directs. Heat figs and syrup to boiling; skim off any froth. Carefully pack figs into hot jars, leaving 1/4-inch head space. Cover with boiling syrup, leaving 1/4-inch head space. Wipe jar rims; seal with hot lids and screw bands. Process 30 minutes in a simmering water bath. Makes about 5 (1-pint) jars.

TIP Dorothy Glover recommends peeling figs for a particularly high-quality jam.

Dorothy Glover   Coushatta, Louisiana   Louisiana State Fair

Sun-Cooked Strawberry Preserves

University English teacher Marilynn Keys selected perfect berries and packed them, one at a time, in jars when she captured the prestigious best of show ribbon with these elegant, fresh-flavored, whole berry preserves. Marilynn Keys sun-cooks her preserves three days, bringing them in at night. In hot, dry Arizona, the process might take only a few hours. For best results, make these preserves when the temperature is in the 80's and relative humidity is less than 60 percent.

5 cups sugar
1/4 cup lemon juice
5 cups washed hulled firm-ripe strawberries

In a large kettle, sprinkle sugar and lemon juice over berries, shaking pan to combine; do not stir. Cover and let stand at room temperature about 1 hour or until sugar is dissolved. Bring mixture to a simmer over medium heat. Cook gently 2 minutes without stirring. Remove from heat, cover and let cool 30 minutes. Pour mixture into shallow glass pans or rigid plastic trays. Syrup should be 1/2 to 3/4 inch deep. Cover with glass or clear plastic film, leaving a 1-inch opening along one side. Place pan in direct sunlight until fruit is plump and syrup thickened to consistency of corn syrup. Occasionally turn berries while sun-cooking. If preserves will be eaten within 1 month, thoroughly wash and scald 4 (1/2-pint) jars. Spoon preserves into hot jars, cover and refrigerate. To process for longer storage or for exhibiting, thoroughly wash and scald 4 (1/2-pint) jars. Keep hot until needed. Prepare lids as manufacturer directs. Carefully drain syrup into a medium-size saucepan and bring to a boil. Pack plumped berries into hot jars. Ladle syrup over berries, leaving 1/4-inch headspace. Wipe jar rims; seal with hot lids and screw bands. Process 10 minutes in a simmering water bath. Makes about 4 (1/2-pint) jars.

Marilynn Keys   Little Rock, Arkansas   Arkansas State Fair

Rosy Tomato & Pineapple Preserves

An enthusiastic competitor since her early days as a tournament tennis player, Sonia Anderson now has turned her competitive energy to preserving. The subtle flavor and rosy color of this tomato-pineapple combination persuaded fair judges that this was best of show for preserves.

2 pounds small firm ripe tomatoes
4 cups sugar
3/4 cup crushed pineapple with juice
1/4 cup lemon juice

Peel tomatoes; cut out stem ends and cores. Cut in quarters. Remove seeds, if desired. Place in a nonmetal bowl, sprinkle with sugar and gently combine. Cover and let stand at least 8 hours, stirring occasionally. Thoroughly wash and scald 4 (1/2-pint) jars. Keep hot until needed. Prepare lids as manufacturer directs. Place a sieve over a large kettle. Drain tomato liquid into kettle. Reserve tomato pulp. Add pineapple with juice and lemon juice to tomato juice. Bring to a boil, stirring frequently. Cook to 220F (105C). Add reserved tomato pulp; boil until thickened. Test with Plate Test, page 180. Remove from heat. Ladle hot mixture into hot jars, leaving 1/4-inch headspace. Wipe jar rims; seal with hot lids and screw bands. Process 10 minutes in a simmering water bath. Makes 4 (1/2-pint) jars.

Sonia Anderson   Alameda, California   California State Fair

VARIATION   To make *Yellow Tomato Preserves*, which won a blue ribbon for Wanda Schmidt across the continent, substitute 2 pounds small, firm, ripe yellow tomatoes for red tomatoes. Then Miss Schmidt recommends, "proceed with tender loving care."

Wanda A. Schmidt   Stockton, New Jersey Flemington (NJ) Agricultural Fair

Strawberry-Walnut Conserve

Marie Carlson started making pickles and preserves when she moved where she could buy tree-ripened fruit and just-picked vegetables from nearby farms. She believes her old-fashioned enamel kettle maintains the most even temperature for making this elegant, flavorful conserve.

2 kiwifruit
4 cups strawberries, washed, hulled
4 cups sugar
1/2 cup lemon juice
1/4 cup kirsch
1 cup walnuts, coarsely chopped

Peel kiwi; crush with potato masher. In a large kettle, combine kiwifruit, strawberries and sugar. Bring to a boil. Cook over medium heat 10 minutes, stirring frequently to keep from sticking. Add lemon juice, kirsch and walnuts. Continue to cook at a rolling boil about 30 minutes or until conserve thickens, stirring constantly. Meanwhile, thoroughly wash and scald 6 (1-pint) jars. Keep hot until needed. Prepare lids as manufacturer directs. Remove conserve from heat. Immediately ladle into hot jars, leaving 1/4-inch headspace. Wipe jar rims; seal with hot lids and screw bands. Process 10 minutes in a simmering water bath. Makes 5 to 6 (1-pint) jars.

Marie L. Carlson   Woodacre, California   California State Fair

Strawberry-Pineapple Conserve

Preserves have to look as good as they taste to win blue ribbons. So Stella Marquand exhibits her most attractive products, like this colorful conserve. She recommends making this on a day when the humidity isn't too high.

3 pints strawberries, washed, hulled
1 medium-size orange
2 cups crushed pineapple, drained
1 cup golden raisins
About 8 cups sugar

Thoroughly wash and scald 6 (1/2-pint) jars. Keep hot until needed. Prepare lids as manufacturer directs. Crush strawberries with a potato masher or chop in a food processor. Quarter orange, remove seeds and grind with peel in a food grinder. Measure prepared fruit, pineapple and raisins; you should have about 8 cups. In a large kettle, combine fruit with an equal amount of sugar. Bring to a boil over medium-high heat, stirring until sugar dissolves. Cook about 20 minutes or until mixture is thick and begins to look transparent, stirring frequently. Test with Plate Test, page 180. Remove from heat. Immediately ladle into hot jars, leaving 1/4-inch headspace. Wipe jar rims; seal with hot lids and screw bands. Process 10 minutes in a simmering water bath. Makes 5 to 6 (1/2-pint) jars.

Stella Marquand   Marshall, Missouri   Missouri State Fair

California Dried Apricot Conserve

Judged best of class, this blue ribbon conserve combines dried California fruits and almonds with fresh citrus juices and Amaretto. Cindy Cartt appreciates having the ingredients available year-round.

1/2 pound dried apricots, cut in thin strips
1 cup golden raisins
3 cups water
Additional water
1-1/2 teaspoons grated orange peel
1 cup orange juice, preferably fresh
2 tablespoons lemon juice
2-1/2 cups sugar
1/2 cup blanched slivered almonds
3 tablespoons Amaretto liqueur

In a large bowl, combine apricots, raisins and 3 cups water. Refrigerate and soak overnight to soften. Pour fruit into a medium-size saucepan; add additional water to cover fruit halfway. Simmer, uncovered, about 15 minutes or until fruit is tender. Stir in orange peel and orange and lemon juice; bring to a boil. Add sugar and cook, uncovered, over medium heat 30 to 40 minutes or until thick, stirring frequently. Mix in almonds last 5 minutes of cooking. Meanwhile, thoroughly wash and scald 4 (1/2-pint) jars. Keep hot until needed. Prepare lids as manufacturer directs. Remove conserve from heat and stir in Amaretto. Ladle into hot jars, leaving 1/4-inch head space. Wipe jar rims; seal with hot lids and screw bands. Process 10 minutes in a simmering water bath. Makes about 4 (1/2-pint) jars.

Cindy Cartt   Sacramento, California   California State Fair

Orange Marmalade

Elaine Pretz sees cooking as an art form, along with her weaving and spinning. This attitude shows in the care she takes to make sure her marmalade looks as good as it tastes. She chooses sweet, unblemished oranges that are heavy for their size.

5 medium-size oranges, thoroughly washed
1 medium-size lemon, thoroughly washed
2 to 2-1/2 cups water
1/8 teaspoon baking soda
1 (1-3/4-oz.) box powdered pectin
1/4 cup orange liqueur
6-1/2 cups sugar

Thoroughly wash and scald 7 (1/2-pint) jars. Keep hot until needed. Prepare lids as manufacturer directs. Using a very sharp knife, remove any discolored spots from oranges and lemon. Cut in half lengthwise, then cut a slice off each end. Trim out center pith and membrane. Slice paper thin, removing seeds; slices should be of even size with even proportion of peel to fruit. In a large kettle, gently combine fruit, 2 cups of water and baking soda. Cover and simmer about 20 minutes or until fruit is tender, stirring occasionally, taking care not to break up fruit. Measure 4 cups fruit and liquid. If necessary, add up to 1/2 cup of water. Return fruit and liquid to kettle; stir in pectin and liqueur. Bring to boil over high heat, stirring constantly. Add sugar all at once and bring to a full rolling boil. Boil hard exactly 1 minute. Remove from heat. Skim off foam with metal spoon. Ladle into hot jars, leaving 1/4-inch headspace. Wipe jar rims; seal with hot lids and screw bands. Process 10 minutes in a simmering water bath. Gently tip jars to distribute fruit and liquid evenly for a few days after processing. Marmalade will take up to a week to set. Makes about 7 (1/2-pint) jars.

Elaine Sachse Pretz   Portland, Oregon   Oregon State Fair

Pear Honey

Locally-grown Kieffer pears are Nancy Johnson's choice for her blue ribbon Pear Honey, but any variety that becomes very soft when cooked is suitable. Select juicy, fully-ripe pears for best flavor. Use this sweet spread to glorify hot biscuits or toast.

    5 pounds pears
    Antioxidant Solution, page 178
    10 cups sugar
    2 cups crushed pineapple with juice

Peel and core pears. Immediately drop pears into Antioxidant Solution. Using coarse blade of a food grinder or in a blender or food processor, chop well-drained pears. In a large heavy kettle, combine pears, sugar and pineapple with juice. Cook, uncovered, over medium heat about 1 hour or until mixture is thick and pears are translucent, stirring frequently to keep mixture from sticking. Meanwhile, thoroughly wash and scald 7 (1-pint) jars. Keep hot until needed. Prepare lids as manufacturer directs. Ladle honey into hot jars, leaving 1/4-inch head space. Wipe jar rims; seal with hot lids and screw bands. Process 10 minutes in a simmering water bath. Makes about 7 (1-pint) jars.

Nancy Johnson   Clever, Missouri   Missouri State Fair

Deanna's Pear Honey

Deanna Little likes to try out new recipes, then makes changes until she has developed her own special version. Her silky-smooth pear honey, enhanced with a touch of lime, is not quite as sweet as the traditional version.

9 cups peeled cored coarsely chopped juicy-ripe
   pears (about 3 pounds)
1-1/2 cups drained crushed pineapple
Grated peel 2 limes
Juice 1 lime
5 cups sugar

Thoroughly wash and scald 8 (1/2-pint) jars. Keep hot until needed. Prepare lids as manufacturer directs. In a large kettle, combine pears, pineapple, lime peel and juice and sugar. Heat to boiling, stirring constantly. Reduce heat to low. Simmer about 20 minutes or until mixture is thick, stirring frequently to prevent sticking. Press mixture through a sieve; reheat. Ladle into hot jars, leaving 1/4-inch head space. Wipe jar rims; seal with hot lids and screw bands. Process 10 minutes in a simmering water bath. Makes 7 to 8 (1/2-pint) jars.

Deanna K. Little   Albuquerque, New Mexico   New Mexico State Fair

PICKLES & CONDIMENTS

The blue ribbon pickle and relish recipes in this book range from ones that a novice can make, such as Dill Bean Pickles, Corn Relish or Bread & Butter Pickles, to more challenging and time-consuming ones, such as Old Fashioned Brined Dill Pickles or Elegant Hot Dog Relish.

But even the recipes that take more skill are not difficult if you observe the #1 rule of pickle making: READ THE RECIPE IN ADVANCE. Otherwise you may discover the pickles you plan to put up today before you leave town for the weekend take four days to make. Make pickles or other products that need time to develop flavor far enough in advance so they will be ready for tasting.

The #2 rule is to use trustworthy, contemporary recipes or heirloom recipes that have been updated to meet today's standards of food safety.

Proportions of vegetable and fruit to vinegar, salt, sugar and spices effect keeping quality as well as flavor of pickles and relishes. Heat processing in a water-bath canner is recommended to destroy the yeasts, molds and bacteria that can cause spoilage and the enzymes that will affect quality of the product. Heat processing also helps assure a good seal on the jar.

Research by food scientists at the University of Minnesota finds that simmering water (200F/94C-205F/96C) will destroy undesirable organisms in cucumber pickles. Older sources continue to call for boiling temperatures for all pickles. See Water-Bath Canner, page 180.

Ingredients

Cucumbers—Small, thin-skinned, warty pickling cucumbers are the choice for pickles. They should be used right after harvesting or chilled and processed within 24 hours. Since the pickling varieties don't keep growing, you may not be able to tell maturity by size. Sort them and use over-mature picklers for eating fresh.

You *can* get by using small to medium-size slicing cucumbers in relishes or even to make bread and butter pickles if picklers are not available.

If your only choice is waxed cucumbers from the grocery store, make something other than cucumber pickles instead.

Vinegar—Commercial jug vinegars are all within the four- to six-percent acetic acid range necessary for pickles. Vinegar is one ingredient where fancy quality isn't better. Homemade wine vinegar and some specialty vinegars may not be high enough in acetic acid.

You can use either distilled white vinegar—sharper flavored, but won't change the color of your product—or the darker, more mellow apple cider vinegar. Distilled vinegar with cider flavor and color also is available.

Salt—Use pickling (canning) salt or Kosher salt. Neither has iodine or anticaking agents that can cause cloudiness and darkening.

Water—If water is very hard, especially if it also has a high iron content, it can cause pickles to discolor. Use soft water, if possible, or bottled distilled water.

Spices—Whole spices will keep pickles and syrup from darkening, when this is important to the appearance of the product. All spices should be fresh to prevent a musty "off" flavor in pickles.

Equipment

Many pickle and relish recipes require big containers for brining and mixing and a six- to eight-quart preserving kettle. *Do not* use galvanized, copper or iron utensils, which can be dangerous, as well as causing undesirable flavor and color changes. *Do* choose stoneware crocks or bowls, glass, stainless steel or food-grade polyethylene plastic containers for mixing and brining and unchipped enamelware or stainless steel kettles for cooking the mixtures.

An accurate kitchen scale is handy, since recipes may call for some ingredients by weight rather than measure.

Canning Jars

Standard tempered-glass canning jars and two-piece lids are required for fair exhibiting and are best to use for all canning. Discard jars that are chipped or cracked. They may not seal or may break. Because pickles are processed in simmering hot water, jars and lids do not need to be sterilized, but they must be thoroughly washed, scalded and kept hot before filling. They also can be put through a complete dishwasher cycle; then kept hot.

Whole Peach Pickles

Nancy Johnson has been canning since she started in 4-H Club projects when she was 10. Her Whole Peach Pickles are made by a two-step method, letting the fruit stand in the pickling syrup over night before processing. This keeps the peaches plump and flavorful. Select firm-ripe fruit that will fit into wide-mouth canning jars.

8 pounds small to medium-size peaches
1 gallon Acidulated Water Solution, page 178
6 cups sugar
4 cups distilled white vinegar
4 (3-inch) sticks cinnamon
2 tablespoons whole cloves, crushed
1 tablespoon ginger

Peel peaches, dropping directly into Acidulated Water Solution to prevent browning. In a large kettle, dissolve sugar in vinegar and bring to a boil. Boil 5 minutes. Skim off foam with a metal spoon. Tie cinnamon, cloves and ginger loosely in cheesecloth; drop into kettle. Rinse peaches in fresh water and drain well. Drop into boiling syrup. Simmer, uncovered, about 5 minutes or just until they can be pierced with a fork. Remove kettle from heat. Cover and let stand in syrup overnight to plump. Thoroughly wash and rinse 4 (1-quart) wide-mouth jars. Keep hot in simmering water until needed. Prepare lids as manufacturer directs. Bring syrup to a boil. Discard spice bag, reserving cinnamon sticks. Carefully arrange peaches in hot jars, leaving 1/2-inch headspace. Place 1 stick of cinnamon in each jar. Cover with boiling syrup, leaving 1/4-inch headspace. Remove air bubbles by running a table knife around inside edge of jar. Wipe jar rims; seal with hot lids and screw bands. Process 20 minutes in a boiling water bath. For best flavor, store in a cool, dark place 1 month before serving. Makes 3 to 4 (1-quart) jars.

Nancy Johnson   Clever, Missouri   Missouri State Fair

Pickled Figs

Tart, sweet Pickled Figs are just one of the many homemade jams, relishes and pickles Irene Hawes puts up to serve when she entertains. As she makes them, she also strives for blue ribbon results at the largest county fair in the world. Picking uniform, unblemished figs with good color and packing picture-perfect jars help her achieve her remarkable success.

4 quarts firm ripe figs, washed, stems trimmed
5 cups sugar
2 quarts water
2 (3-inch) sticks cinnamon
1 tablespoon whole cloves
1 tablespoon whole allspice
3 cups vinegar

Peel figs or use unpeeled, if desired. In a large container, pour boiling water over figs. Let stand until cool; drain. In a large kettle, combine 3 cups of sugar and water. Cook until sugar dissolves, stirring constantly. Add figs and simmer slowly 30 minutes. Tie cinnamon, cloves and allspice into cheesecloth. Add to figs along with remaining 2 cups of sugar and vinegar. Cook gently until figs are clear. Remove from heat. Let stand in a cool place 12 to 24 hours. Thoroughly wash and scald 8 (1-pint) jars. Keep hot until needed. Prepare lids as manufacturer directs. Discard spice bag. Heat figs and syrup to simmering. Carefully pack figs into hot jars, leaving 1/4-inch headspace. Cover with hot syrup, leaving 1/4-inch headspace. Remove air bubbles by running a table knife around inside edge of jar. Wipe jar rims; seal with hot lids and screw bands. Process 15 minutes in a boiling water bath. Makes about 8 (1-pint) jars.

Irene Hawes   Ontario, California   Los Angeles County Fair

Easy Spiced Pear Pickles

Mary Ann Hildreth puts up extra jars of Bartlett pears every summer to transform into her elegant fruit pickles. Although she has to reprocess them to exhibit at the Ohio State Fair, for home use they need only be refrigerated. If you can't start with your own prize-winning canned pears, buy a top-quality brand for perfect halves that will keep their shape.

3 quarts home-canned Bartlett pears or 3 (19-ounce) cans pears
2 cups distilled white vinegar
6 cups sugar
2 teaspoons whole cloves
1 slice gingerroot or 1 teaspoon ground ginger
3 (3-inch) sticks cinnamon

🎗Drain pears. In a medium-size saucepan, combine pear juice, vinegar and sugar. Tie cloves, gingerroot and cinnamon into cheesecloth. Add to pear juice mixture. Bring to a boil, stirring constantly. Then simmer, uncovered, about 8 minutes, stirring occasionally. Carefully arrange pear halves in a crock or large bowl. Pour hot syrup over pears. Let stand overnight. For home use, discard spice bag and refrigerate pears in syrup at least 3 days before serving. Store in refrigerator up to several weeks. To process, sterilize 4 (1-pint) jars. Keep hot until needed. Prepare lids as manufacturer directs. Discard spice bag. Carefully drain syrup from pears into a large saucepan. Heat to boiling. Arrange well-drained pears in hot jars. Cover with hot syrup, leaving 1/2-inch headspace. Wipe jar rims; seal with hot lids and screw bands. Process 20 minutes in a boiling water bath. Makes about 4 (1-pint) jars.

Mary Ann Hildreth   Fairborn, Ohio   Ohio State Fair

Linda's Famous Okra Pickles

Colleagues at Northrop Services, Environmental Services have followed the saga of Linda Cooper's attempts to perfect her Okra Pickles in the company newspaper. Finally, after 5 years of experimenting, this recipe—made with her organically-grown okra—was awarded the blue ribbon at the 1986 state fair. Will she try again? The "Northrop News" will report. A favorite snack food of many Southerners, well-made okra pickles are crisp, a characteristic Northerners do not usually associate with this vegetable.

3-1/2 pounds uniformly small okra pods, washed, well drained
6 cloves garlic
6 hot peppers or to taste
4 tablespoons mustard seed
2 stalks celery, cut in 6 (2-inch) pieces
2 cups distilled white vinegar
4 cups water
2 teaspoons dill seed
1/3 cup pickling salt

Sterilize 6 (1-pint) jars. Keep hot until needed. Prepare lids as manufacturer directs. Pack okra firmly into hot jars, leaving 1/2-inch headspace. Add 1 clove of garlic, 1 or more hot peppers, 2 teaspoons of mustard seed and 1 piece of celery to each jar. In a large saucepan, combine vinegar, water, dill seed and salt. Heat to boiling. Pour boiling liquid over okra, leaving 1/4-inch headspace. Wipe jar rims; seal with hot lids and screw bands. Process 10 minutes in a boiling water bath. Makes 6 (1-pint) jars.

Linda Cooper   Chapel Hill, North Carolina   North Carolina State Fair

Old-Fashioned Brined Dill Pickles

Genuine dill pickles have a characteristic flavor impossible to duplicate except by a lengthy fermentation process. Wanda Schmidt has the advantage of years of experience as an expert pickle maker. But anyone who follows her directions carefully can take advantage of her expertise and have the satisfaction of making "real" dill pickles. Young pickling cucumbers, freshly harvested, are essential.

20 to 30 Brined Pickles
2 tablespoons salt
1/2 cup sugar
3 cups vinegar
3 cups water
2 tablespoons mixed pickling spices, tied in cheesecloth
4 heads fresh dill

<u>*Brined Pickles*</u>

20 to 30 uniformly sized
  pickling-cucumbers
  (about 4 inches long)
1/3 cup whole mixed pickling spices
1 large bunch fresh dill
1 cup vinegar
1 gallon water
3/4 cup pickling salt

Prepare Brined Pickles. Thoroughly wash and scald 4 (1-quart) jars. Keep hot until needed. Prepare lids as manufacturer directs. In a large saucepan, combine salt, sugar, vinegar, water and spice bag. Bring to a boil over high heat, stirring constantly. Reduce heat and simmer 15 minutes. Discard spice bag. Pack pickles and dill into hot jars, leaving 1/4-inch headspace. Pour hot liquid over pickles, leaving 1/4-inch headspace. Wipe jar rims; seal with hot lids and screw bands. Process 15 minutes in a simmering water bath. Makes about 4 (1-quart) jars.

Brined Pickles

Thoroughly scrub a 3- or 4-gallon crock. Scrub cucumbers with a brush, removing blossom end. Sprinkle half of pickling spices on bottom of crock. Cover with a layer of dill. Add cucumbers to within 4 inches of top of crock. In a large container, mix vinegar, water and salt until salt dissolves. Pour over cucumbers. Place remaining pickling spices and another layer of dill on top. Cover with a clean heavy plate to hold cucumbers under brine. Weight plate with a jar filled with water, if necessary. Do not overfill crock. Water will be drawn from cucumbers during brining process. Store container at 65F(19C) to 70F(21C), if possible. Every day remove scum that forms, but do not stir up brine. In about 2 weeks, test a pickle by cutting and tasting it. It should have a good dill flavor and be clear all the way through with no white spots. If not, let pickles frement up to 1 week longer and retest. Drain pickles; clean crock. Return pickles to crock. Cover with cold water. Soak 24 hours, changing water every 8 hours to remove salt.

VARIATION To make garlic dill pickles, add 4 large peeled cloves garlic to pickling solution. Pack 1 clove garlic into each jar.

Wanda A. Schmidt Stockton, New Jersey Flemington (NJ) Agricultural Fair

Bread & Butter Pickles

At 80, Melanie Robichaux is still winning blue ribbons for her pickles. In 26 years of exhibiting, she has collected well over 1000 ribbons from state and parish fairs and says she has lost track of the number of times she has been overall winner in canning. This recipe for Bread & Butter Pickles is one of her favorites and one of the easiest for a novice pickler to make.

3 pounds medium-size cucumbers
2 large white onions, chopped
1/2 large red bell pepper, washed, seeded, chopped
2 tablespoons pickling salt
1-1/4 cups cider vinegar
1-1/4 cups sugar
1-1/2 teaspoons mustard seed
1 teaspoon tumeric
1/8 teaspoon ground cloves

Scrub cucumbers with a brush. Cut off and discard a thin slice from each end. Using a sharp knife, slice cucumbers as thin as possible or slice in a food processor. Layer cucumbers, onions and pepper in a large bowl, sprinkling salt on each layer. Cover and let stand 1 hour. Thoroughly wash and scald 4 (1-pint) jars. Keep hot until needed. Prepare lids as manufacturer directs. Drain vegetables; rinse in cold water and drain thoroughly. In a large kettle, heat vinegar, sugar, mustard seed, tumeric and cloves until sugar is dissolved, stirring constantly. Bring to a boil. Add vegetables and heat, but do not boil. Remove from heat. Immediately pack vegetables into hot jars, leaving 1/4-inch headspace. Pour hot syrup over vegetables, leaving 1/4-inch headspace. Wipe jar rims; seal with hot lids and screw bands. Process 5 minutes in a simmering water bath. Makes about 4 (1-pint) jars.

Melanie Robichaux   Alexandria, Louisiana   Louisiana State Fair

Mrs. Robichaux's
Sweet Cucumber Pickles

Two essential ingredients for making Melanie Robichaux's prize-winning sweet four-day pickles are patience and young pickling cucumbers, freshly picked.

1 gallon young pickling cucumbers (about 3 inches long)
1 cup pickling salt
1 gallon water
6 cups sugar
6 cups cider vinegar
1 cup water
1 tablespoon mixed pickling spices tied loosely in cheesecloth

Scrub cucumbers with a brush to clean and remove spines. Remove blossom ends. Place in a crock or a large stainless steel or enamelware kettle. In a large container, dissolve pickling salt in 1 gallon water. Cover cucumbers with brine. Top with a weighted plate to keep cucumbers covered with brine, if necessary. Let stand 24 hours. Drain cucumbers, rinse in fresh water and drain again. In a large stainless steel or enamelware kettle, combine 3 cups of sugar, vinegar, 1 cup water and spice bag. Bring to boiling, stirring constantly. Reduce heat, cover and simmer 30 minutes. Meanwhile, puncture each cucumber with tines of a fork. Add cucumbers to syrup. Simmer 15 minutes. Remove from heat. Cover and let cucumbers stand in syrup at room temperature 48 hours. Thoroughly wash and scald 8 (1-pint) jars. Keep hot until needed. Prepare lids as manufacturer directs. Drain cucumbers thoroughly, reserving syrup. Add remaining 3 cups of sugar to syrup. Heat to boiling. Reduce heat and simmer 5 minutes, stirring frequently. Discard spice bag. Pack drained pickles into hot jars, leaving 1/2-inch headspace. Cover with hot syrup, leaving 1/4-inch headspace. Remove air bubbles by running a table knife inside edge of jar. Wipe jar rims; seal with hot lids and screw bands. Process 10 minutes in a simmering water bath. Makes about 8 (1-pint) jars.

Melanie Robichaux   Alexandria, Louisiana   Louisiana State Fair

Pickled Beets

A "country cook" who learned her skills from her grandmother, Loraine LaPole knows fresh-picked flavor makes a difference even with a sturdy vegetable like beets. She selects tender, young beets of similar size and cooks them with root ends and some stem attached, so they will retain their dark red color.

6 to 7 pounds uniformly small beets, well scrubbed
1-1/2 cups water
3-1/2 cups cider vinegar
1-3/4 cups granulated sugar
1/4 cup firmly packed brown sugar
1-1/2 teaspoons salt
4 teaspoons whole allspice
2 (3-inch) sticks cinnamon

Trim off all but 2 inches of each beet stem, leaving root end. In a large kettle, add beets and just enough water to cover beets. Cover and cook about 25 minutes or until tender-firm. Meanwhile, thoroughly wash and scald 6 (1-pint) jars. Keep hot until needed. Prepare lids as manufacturer directs. Drain beets; cover with cold water. Cool enough to slip off skins; drain. Remove skins. Meanwhile, in a large kettle, combine 1-1/2 cups water, vinegar, sugars, salt, allspice and cinnamon. Stir over low heat until sugar is dissolved. Add beets, cover and simmer 15 minutes. Remove from heat; discard cinnamon sticks. Using a slotted spoon, pack hot beets and some of allspice into hot jars, leaving 1/2-inch headspace. Pour hot liquid over beets, leaving 1/2-inch headspace. Remove air bubbles by running a table knife inside edge of jar. Wipe jar rims; seal with hot lids and screw bands. Process 30 minutes in a boiling water bath. Makes 6 (1-pint) jars.

Loraine LaPole   Anderson, Indiana   Indiana State Fair

Dill Bean Pickles

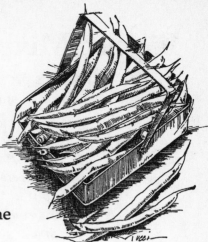

Mom's bean pickles are a great favorite in the Wolkerstorfer family, where the children prefer them to buttered beans or to dill pickles. For a crisp product, pick beans at a slightly firmer stage than for eating and process immediately. Veronica Wolkerstorfer prefers wide-mouth pint jars, so she can pack the beans lengthwise.

2 pounds green beans, washed, trimmed to same length
1 teaspoon cayenne pepper
4 cloves garlic
4 heads fresh dill
2-1/2 cups water
2-1/2 cups distilled white vinegar
1/4 cup pickling salt

Thoroughly wash and scald 4 (1-pint) jars. Keep hot until needed. Prepare lids as manufacturer directs. Pack beans, lengthwise, into hot jars, leaving 1/4-inch headspace. Add 1/4 teaspoon of cayenne pepper, 1 clove of garlic and 1 head of dill to each jar. In a medium-size kettle, combine water, vinegar and salt. Heat to boiling. Pour boiling hot liquid over beans, leaving 1/4-inch headspace. Wipe jar rims; seal with hot lids and screw bands. Process 10 minutes in a boiling water bath. Dill Bean Pickles are ready to eat in 2 weeks. Makes about 4 (1-pint) jars.

Veronica Wolkerstorfer   Maplewood, Minnesota   Minnesota State Fair

Pickled Mixed Vegetables

Fair judges pronounced Janice White's colorful layered pickled vegetables best of show and awarded her a sweepstakes ribbon.

3 medium-size carrots, peeled, cut in 1/4-inch slices
1 small bunch broccoli, washed, broken in flowerets, stems trimmed
3 red bell peppers, washed, seeded, cut in 1-inch-wide strips
4 (2 inches in diameter) onions, peeled, cut in 1/2-inch slices
3 (2 inches in diameter) cucumbers, washed, unpeeled, cut in
  1/4-inch slices
1 small firm cauliflower, washed, broken in flowerets,
  stems trimmed
1 cup pickling salt
4 quarts water
1/4 cup mustard seed
2 tablespoons celery seed
1 hot red pepper
2 cups sugar
6-1/2 cups distilled white vinegar

Place vegetables in a large bowl. In another large bowl, dissolve salt in water. Pour over vegetables. Cover and let stand 8 hours in a cool place or refrigerate overnight. Thoroughly wash and scald 3 wide-mouth (1-quart) jars. Keep hot until needed. Prepare lids as manufacturer directs. Drain vegetables, rinse and thoroughly drain again. Tie mustard and celery seeds and red pepper into cheesecloth. In a medium-size saucepan, bring spice bag, sugar and vinegar to a boil. Reduce heat. Simmer 15 minutes, stirring occasionally. Using long tweezers, pack vegetables tightly into each hot jar in this order: 3 rows of carrots; 1 (3/4-inch) layer of broccoli flowerets; 1 layer of overlapping bell pepper strips; 1 layer of sliced onions; and 2 layers of cucumber slices. Fill jar with cauliflower pieces, leaving 1/2-inch headspace. Discard spice bag. Pour simmering-hot syrup over vegetables, leaving 1/4-inch headspace. Remove air bubbles by running a table knife inside edge of jar. Wipe jar rims; seal with hot lids and screw bands.

Process 20 minutes in a boiling water bath. Or for a quick version, vegetables can be mixed together, rather than layered, and processed in 6 (1-pint) jars 15 minutes. Makes 3 (1-quart) jars or 6 (1-pint) jars.

Janice White   Everett, Washington   Evergreen (Washington) State Fair

Dilled Green Tomatoes

Helen Kirsch retires a recipe from fair competition after it has received a blue ribbon, but these attractive and unusual pickles will continue to brighten family meals. For crisp pickles, tomatoes must be green all the way through.

72 (2- to 2-1/2 inch) firm green tomatoes, washed
3-1/2 cups distilled white vinegar
3-1/2 cups water
1/4 cup pickling salt
1 large green bell pepper, washed, seeded, cut in 12 (1/2-inch) strips
1 large red bell pepper, washed, seeded, cut in 12 (1/2-inch) strips
3 stalks celery, cut in 6 (4-inch) pieces
6 cloves garlic
3/4 cup dill seed

Thoroughly wash and scald 6 (1-pint) jars. Keep hot until needed. Prepare lids as manufacturer directs. Core tomatoes; set aside. In a medium-size saucepan, combine vinegar, water and salt; bring to a boil. Pack about 10 to 12 tomatoes into each hot jar, leaving 1/2-inch headspace. Arrange 2 strips each of green and red bell peppers, 1 piece of celery and 1 clove of garlic in each jar so they are visible. Add 2 tablespoons of dill seeds to each jar. Pour boiling liquid over tomatoes, leaving 1/2-inch headspace. Wipe jar rims; seal with hot lids and screw bands. Process 15 minutes in a boiling water bath. Tomatoes are ready to eat in 4 to 6 weeks. Makes 6 (1-pint) jars.

Helen Kirsch   Albuquerque, New Mexico   New Mexico State Fair

Watermelon Rind Pickles Pretz

Orange slices are an unusual and attractive addition to Elaine Pretz' slightly sweet, spicy pickles. The two-day process lets the pickles absorb more syrup and makes them tender but crisp.

1 watermelon rind
1 cup pickling salt
2 quarts cold water
1 tablespoon whole cloves
5 (3-inch) sticks cinnamon
1 tablespoon whole allspice
6 cups sugar
4 cups white vinegar
2 cups water
5 oranges, thinly sliced, seeded, end pieces discarded
6 (3-inch) sticks cinnamon, if desired

Remove all pink flesh and green skin of watermelon rind. Cut pieces about 1-1/2 inches long and as wide as rind is thick. Measure 4 quarts rind. Place rind in a crock. Dissolve salt in 2 quarts cold water and pour over rind; keep rind fully covered. Soak 8 hours or overnight. Sterilize 6 (1-pint) jars. Keep hot until needed. Prepare lids as manufacturer directs. Drain and rinse rind thoroughly with cold running water. In a large kettle, cover rind with water and bring to a boil. Reduce heat to low. Simmer about 10 minutes or until rind is just crisp-tender. Drain thoroughly; set aside. Wash kettle. Tie cloves, cinnamon and allspice in cheesecloth. In washed kettle, combine spice bag, sugar, vinegar, and 2 cups water. Heat to boiling and cook 5 minutes or until mixture is slightly thickened. Add rind and orange slices. Simmer 10 to 15 minutes or until melon pieces are clear. Remove from heat. Discard spice bag and let rind cool in syrup to plump up. Bring back to boiling. Carefully pack melon pieces and orange slices into hot jars. Add 1 stick of cinnamon to each jar, if desired. Cover with boiling syrup, leaving 1/4-inch headspace. Wipe jar rims; seal with hot lids and screw bands. Process 20 minutes in a boiling water bath. Makes 6 (1-pint) jars.

Elaine Sachse Pretz   Portland, Oregon   Oregon State Fair

Corn Relish

Mary Heying is a great-grandmother who has been cooking and preserving food since she was nine years old. Although canning is second nature to her by now, she still works at making every jar look as attractive as possible. The corn in her relish is bright and crisp; bits of green and red pepper add color. Easy enough for a novice canner, this old favorite relish is a welcome addition to almost any menu.

20 medium-size ears of corn, husks and silk removed
1 cup diced green bell pepper
1 cup diced red bell pepper
1 cup diced onion
1 cup diced celery
1 tablespoon salt
2 cups sugar
2 tablespoons mustard seed
1 teaspoon celery seed
1/2 teaspoon tumeric
2 cups water
2-1/2 cups distilled white vinegar

Thoroughly wash and scald 6 (1-pint) jars. Keep hot until needed. Prepare lids as manufacturer directs. In a large kettle, boil ears of corn 5 minutes. Drop into ice water; cool 5 minutes. Carefully cut kernels from cob (do not scrape cobs). Measure 10 cups corn. In a large kettle, combine corn with remaining ingredients. Boil gently, uncovered, 15 minutes. Remove from heat. Ladle into hot jars, leaving 1/4-inch headspace. Wipe jar rims; seal with hot lids and screw bands. Process 15 minutes in a boiling water bath. Makes 5 to 6 (1-pint) jars.

Mary Heying   Miami, Missouri   Missouri State Fair

Red Cherry Conserve-Relish

When retired English professor Travis Trittschuh moved from Detroit to Utah, where he could raise his own fruit and vegetables, he found he enjoyed canning and drying his produce. His tart-sweet relish includes a combination of fruits and nuts, typical of a conserve. Then he adds vinegar and turns it into a rich-flavored relish to serve with poultry or pork. He prefers to cook it very slowly for several hours. Less patient preservers may reduce the cooking time.

3 cups pitted sour cherries, coarsely chopped
1-1/2 cups raisins
1-1/2 teaspoons ground cinnamon
1/2 teaspoon ground cloves
1 cup honey
1 cup granulated sugar
1 cup firmly packed brown sugar
1 cup distilled white vinegar
1-1/2 cups chopped pecans

In a large kettle, combine all ingredients except pecans. Bring to a boil over medium heat, stirring constantly. Reduce heat to simmer. Cook about 2 hours or until mixture is thickened to desired consistency, stirring occasionally. Meanwhile, thoroughly wash and scald 6 (1/2-pint) jars. Prepare lids as manufacturer directs. Stir pecans into cherry mixture; simmer a few minutes longer. Remove from heat. Immediately ladle into hot jars, leaving 1/4-inch headspace. Wipe jar rims; seal with hot lids and screw bands. Process 10 minutes in a simmering water bath. Makes 6 (1/2-pint) jars.

Travis Trittschuh Moab, Utah   Utah State Fair

Dixie Relish

Maybeth Wilson's eye-catching relish stands out because of its bright color and crisp texture. Instead of grinding the vegetables, she chops them by hand with a special cutter, so each one retains its identity.

> 1/4 cup pickling salt
> 2 quarts cold water
> 4 cups chopped cabbage
> 2 cups chopped white onions
> 2 cups chopped red bell peppers
> 2 cups chopped green bell peppers
> 3/4 cup sugar
> 1/4 cup mustard seed
> 2 tablespoons celery seed
> 4 cups cider vinegar

In a large bowl, dissolve salt in water. Stir in cabbage, onions and bell peppers. Let stand at room temperature 3 hours. Drain thoroughly. In a medium-size bowl, combine sugar, mustard and celery seeds and vinegar, stirring until sugar dissolves. Pour over vegetables. Let stand overnight. Thoroughly wash and scald 4 (1-pint) jars. Keep hot until needed. Prepare lids as manufacturer directs. In a large kettle, bring vegetables and liquid to boiling, stirring occasionally. Remove from heat. Immediately ladle into hot jars, leaving 1/4-inch headspace. Remove air bubbles by running a table knife inside edge of jar. Wipe jar rims; seal with hot lids and screw bands. Process 15 minutes in a simmering water bath. Makes 3 to 4 (1-pint) jars.

Maybeth J. Wilson   Marion, Louisiana   Louisiana State Fair

Elegant Hot Dog Relish

Jan Wagner's mustardy relish is like a premium version of the commercial product.

13 medium-size cucumbers, washed, finely chopped
3 red bell peppers, washed, seeded, finely chopped
6 green bell peppers, washed, seeded, finely chopped
1 extra-large sweet onion, finely chopped
1 gallon water
1/4 cup pickling salt
4 cups distilled white vinegar
2 cups water
6 cups sugar
4 teaspoons mustard seed
4 teaspoons celery seed
1 (15-1/4-oz.) can crushed pineapple
2 tablespoons dry mustard
1 tablespoon turmeric
1 cup all-purpose flour

Combine vegetables in a large bowl. Mix 1 gallon water and pickling salt; pour over vegetables. Let stand overnight. Thoroughly wash and scald 11 (1-pint) jars. Keep hot until needed. Prepare lids as manufacturer directs. In a large kettle, bring vegetables and water to a boil. Drain vegetables thoroughly. Wash kettle; combine vegetables, vinegar, 2 cups water, sugar and mustard and celery seeds. Bring to a boil, stirring occasionally. Meanwhile, drain pineapple juice into a glass measure, reserving fruit. In a small bowl, mix dry mustard, tumeric and flour. Using a wire whisk, slowly add pineapple juice and enough liquid from hot vegetable mixture to make a thin smooth paste. Carefully add mustard paste, a little at a time, to hot vegetable mixture, stirring constantly. Stir in reserved pineapple. Simmer until relish has thickened slightly, stirring constantly. Remove from heat. Immediately ladle into hot jars, leaving 1/4-inch headspace. Wipe jar rims; seal with hot lids and screw bands. Process 10 minutes in a simmering water bath. Makes 11 (1-pint) jars.

Jan Wagner   Salem, Oregon   Oregon State Fair

Plum BBQ Sauce

Glorify ribs, chicken or franks with this dark, slightly sweet barbecue sauce. Karla Dellner prefers to use Satsuma plums or the more available Santa Rosas.

5 pounds plums, washed, pitted, cut in quarters
4 cups medium-dry red wine
2-1/2 cups chopped onions
2 cloves garlic, minced
Grated peel 1 lemon
Juice and pulp 1 lemon
2 (8-oz.) cans tomato sauce
1-1/2 cups molasses
1-1/4 cups firmly packed brown sugar
2 tablespoons Worcestershire sauce
2 tablespoons prepared mustard
1/2 cup cider vinegar
2 teaspoons salt
1 teaspoon black pepper
1 teaspoon ground red pepper
1 teaspoon ginger

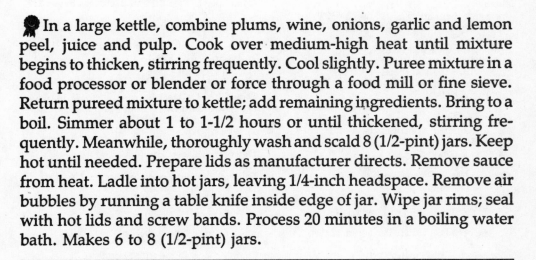

In a large kettle, combine plums, wine, onions, garlic and lemon peel, juice and pulp. Cook over medium-high heat until mixture begins to thicken, stirring frequently. Cool slightly. Puree mixture in a food processor or blender or force through a food mill or fine sieve. Return pureed mixture to kettle; add remaining ingredients. Bring to a boil. Simmer about 1 to 1-1/2 hours or until thickened, stirring frequently. Meanwhile, thoroughly wash and scald 8 (1/2-pint) jars. Keep hot until needed. Prepare lids as manufacturer directs. Remove sauce from heat. Ladle into hot jars, leaving 1/4-inch headspace. Remove air bubbles by running a table knife inside edge of jar. Wipe jar rims; seal with hot lids and screw bands. Process 20 minutes in a boiling water bath. Makes 6 to 8 (1/2-pint) jars.

Karla Dellner   Cameron Park, California   California State Fair

Index

CONTRIBUTORS OF BLUE RIBBON WINNING RECIPES

Anderson, Kenneth
Anderson, Sonia
Ashburn, Ramona G.
Baldwin, Elva
Belden, Ruth
Blesener, Nadine
Bond, Mele
Bouffard, Carla
Boyers, Lynne
Bradow, Vandy
Byrd, Betsy
Canady, Harvey
Carlson, Marie L.
Cartt, Cindy
Chinick, Evelyn
Collins, Judy Ann
Cooper, Linda
Crawford, Georgia L.
Curley, Diane
Danuser, Brenda
Datko, Rose M.
Davis, Anna Marie
Dellner, Karla
Drews, Kristyn L.
Dubois, Joyce
Dunegan, Shirley
Durrell, Traci
Ebner, Ellen
Elgin, Dot
Falk, Blanche
Faris, Marjorie
Forbis, Lena
Ford, Ruth B.
Glover, Dorothy
Grizel, Jan
Gudat, JoAnne
Hansen, Lucille
Hansen, Sandy
Hawes, Irene
Herzog, Sandra
Hess, Clara
Heying, Mary

Hildreth, Charles
Hildreth, Mary Ann
Holley, Harriet C.
Horst, Debra
Jackson, Amy A.
Janas, Elaine
Jenkins, Marguerite
Jones, Jacqueline
Johnson, Marjorie
Johnson, Nancy
Kerns, Betty
Keys, Marilynn
Kirsch, Helen
Klabunde, Michelle D.
Kopf, Suzanne
Krueger, Ronald P.
Kuntz, Bill
LaPole, Loraine
LaPresle, Sarah
Larson, Joanne
Lawson, Virginia
Leach, Eunice R.
Lillemon, Bonnie
Little, Deanna K.
Livelsberger, Janice
Long, Margaret
Losey, Irene
Lundberg, Ruth
Lutes, Terrill
Malnaa, Lora
Marquand, Stella
Martell, Marilyn
Maurer, Ursula
McAlister, Joy
McGrath, Dorothy
McLain, Rhoda
Mers-Lloyd, Carol Joy
Miller, Dorothy
Mootz, Cecilia A.
Morgan, Donna M.
Moser, Susan C.
Neavoll, Fran

Noltemeyer, Shirley
O'Connell, Dorothy
Parker, Larry R.
Pauls, Linda
Peterson, Fay
Pezzi, Paula
Platt, Timothy
Plowman, Donna
Pretz, Elaine Sachse
Reef, Janelle
Roberts, Judi
Robichaux, Melanie
Rushton, Helen
Schmidt, Wanda A.
Schneiderman, Louise
Schofield, Linda Ann
Schuman, Mary E.
Shaw, Linda G.
Shull, Margo J.
Skeeters, Suzanne R.
Specht, Kathy
Squires, Dawn C.
Stroud, Sherry
Swenson, Gwendolyn
Tarbell, Robin
Taticek, Beth
Tite, Diane L.
Traxler, Leah J.
Trittschuh, Travis
Turnbull, Denise M.
Van de Zande, Derrik
Van de Zande, Paulette
Wagner, Jan
Weakley, Cynthia
Westman, Harriett
White, Janice
Wilson, Maybeth J.
Wolkerstorfer, Veronica
York, Laura Case
York, Martha
Young, Heather

Metric Chart

Comparison to Metric Measure

When You Know	Symbol	Multiply By	To Find	Symbol
teaspoons	tsp	5.0	milliliters	ml
tablespoons	tbsp	15.0	milliliters	ml
fluid ounces	fl. oz.	30.0	milliliters	ml
cups	c	0.24	liters	l
pints	pt.	0.47	liters	l
quarts	qt.	0.95	liters	l
ounces	oz.	28.0	grams	g
pounds	lb.	0.45	kilograms	kg
Fahrenheit	F	5/9 (after subtracting 32)	Celsius	C

Liquid Measure to Milliliters

1/4 teaspoon	=	1.25 milliliters
1/2 teaspoon	=	2.5 milliliters
3/4 teaspoon	=	3.75 milliliters
1 teaspoon	=	5.0 milliliters
1-1/4 teaspoons	=	6.25 milliliters
1-1/2 teaspoons	=	7.5 milliliters
1-3/4 teaspoons	=	8.75 milliliters
2 teaspoons	=	10.0 milliliters
1 tablespoon	=	15.0 milliliters
2 tablespoons	=	30.0 milliliters

Liquid Measure to Liters

1/4 cup	=	0.06 liters
1/2 cup	=	0.12 liters
3/4 cup	=	0.18 liters
1 cup	=	0.24 liters
1-1/4 cups	=	0.3 liters
1-1/2 cups	=	0.36 liters
2 cups	=	0.48 liters
2-1/2 cups	=	0.6 liters
3 cups	=	0.72 liters
3-1/2 cups	=	0.84 liters
4 cups	=	0.96 liters
4-1/2 cups	=	1.08 liters
5 cups	=	1.2 liters
5-1/2 cups	=	1.32 liters

Fahrenheit to Celsius

F	C
200—205	95
220—225	105
245—250	120
275	135
300—305	150
325—330	165
345—350	175
370—375	190
400—405	205
425—430	220
445—450	230
470—475	245
500	260